*By following the perfect model of the Holy Family, our homes will become living torches of God's light.*

—Pope Leo XIV

# 33 DAYS TO NAZARETH JOY

A Consecration *to* Jesus
*Through* the Holy Family

Charlotte Foudy

**33 Days to Nazareth Joy:**
**A Consecration to Jesus Through the Holy Family**
© 2025 Charlotte Foudy

All rights reserved. No part of this book may be reproduced in any form or by any means, electronic or mechanical, including photocopying, recording, or by any information storage and retrieval system, without permission in writing from the author, except for brief quotations used in reviews or scholarly works. For permission requests, contact the publisher at info@sanctorumpress.com.

Scripture quotations are from the Revised Standard Version, Catholic Edition (RSV-CE). Copyright © 1965 and 1966 by the Division of Christian Education of the National Council of the Churches of Christ in the United States of America. Used by permission. All rights reserved.

*Nihil Obstat:* Most Reverend Edgar M. da Cunha, S.D.V., D.D.
*Imprimatur:* Most Reverend Edgar M. da Cunha, S.D.V., D.D., Bishop of Fall River

The *nihil obstat* and *imprimatur* are official declarations that a book or pamphlet is free from doctrinal or moral error. No implication is contained therein that those who grant the *nihil obstat* or *imprimatur* agree with the contents or statements expressed.

ISBN: 979-8-9934483-2-9 (Paperback edition)
ISBN: 979-8-9934483-3-6 (E-book edition)
ISBN: 979-8-9934483-4-3 (Hardback edition)

First Edition: December 2025

Cover design by 2Faced Design
Book design by Angela Grace Morgan | Imprint Media Lab
Copyediting by Damon Friedberg, Jacob Kanclerz, and Melissa Woods

Published by Sanctorum Press
www.sanctorumpress.com

Printed in the United States of America

*To the Holy Family:
Jesus, Mary, and Joseph.
And to my own family,
Mark, Michael, Therese, and Gianna,
whose love has taught me
the meaning of Nazareth.*

# Contents

| | |
|---|---|
| Preface | ix |
| *Litany of the Holy Family* | 3 |
| Introduction | 7 |
| How to Use this Book | 9 |
| Suggested Starting Dates | 13 |

**Preparing the Heart: Foundations of Consecration** — 19
- Foundations of Consecration — 21
- Marian and Holy Family Consecration — 29
- Entering the Hidden Life of Nazareth — 37
- The Family as the Domestic Church — 47
- *Prayer Before the Consecration* — 61

**Week 1: The Call of Mercy** — 63
- Day 1: Mercy at the Heart of the Gospel — 65
- Day 2: Trusting His Providence — 71
- Day 3: The Father's Merciful Heart — 77
- Day 4: Mercy Made Present — 81
- Day 5: The Spirit's Gentle Presence — 87
- Day 6: The Mystery of Love — 93
- Day 7: The Communion of Prayer — 97

**Week 2: The Journey of Faith** — 103
- Day 8: Honoring the Holy Family — 105

| | |
|---|---|
| Day 9: God's Eternal Plan | 111 |
| Day 10: Distinct Roles, One Unity | 117 |
| Day 11: The Holiness of Family Roles | 123 |
| Day 12: Restoring Hope at Home | 129 |
| Day 13: A Family That Reflects God | 135 |
| Day 14: Faith in the Midst of Trials | 141 |
| **Week 3: The Humility of Bethlehem** | **147** |
| Day 15: The Road to Bethlehem | 149 |
| Day 16: Finding God in Rejection | 155 |
| Day 17: God Reveals Himself to the Lowly | 161 |
| Day 18: God's Presence in Poverty | 167 |
| Day 19: Heaven Rejoices on Earth | 173 |
| Day 20: The Visit of the Magi | 179 |
| Day 21: Simeon's Long-Awaited Joy | 185 |
| **Week 4: The Path of Holiness in the Home** | **191** |
| Day 22: God With Us in Exile | 193 |
| Day 23: The Hidden Years | 199 |
| Day 24: Obedience Born of Love | 203 |
| Day 25: Perfect in Love | 209 |
| Day 26: Peace That the World Cannot Give | 215 |
| Day 27: Guardian, Provider, Protector | 221 |
| Day 28: The Steadfast Heart of Mary | 227 |
| **Final Days: The Hearts of Nazareth** | **233** |
| Day 29: The Harmony of Hearts | 235 |
| Day 30: True Riches in Nazareth | 241 |
| Day 31: Hidden Yet Holy | 247 |
| Day 32: Hope Through the Valleys | 253 |

| | |
|---|---|
| Day 33: Under Their Protection | 259 |
| *Consecration Day* | *265* |
| **Living the Consecration: Christ Forge** | **277** |
| Overview | 279 |
| Forged in Love | 281 |
| The Way of the Forge | 285 |
| The Christ Forge Virtues | 289 |
| How to Practice the Forge at Home | 295 |
| *Prayer of Renewal: Lord, Forge Our Hearts in Love* | *299* |
| **Appendices** | **303** |
| Addendum I: A Pilgrimage of the Heart | 305 |
| Addendum II: Family Devotional Prayers | 315 |
| Bibliography | 319 |
| About the Author | 327 |
| Acknowledgments | 328 |
| About Sanctorum Press | 329 |

# Preface

There are days when the cadence of our household feels like it's moving faster than I can keep up. Dishes stack in the sink, clothes spill across the floor, homework covers the table, and schedules overlap in a blur of activity. It feels anything but holy. And yet, holiness is not about perfect order or quiet calm. It is about letting Christ meet us right in the middle of it all.

My own pause comes each Sunday, when, after receiving the Eucharist, I slip into the chapel to pray. I say this each week: "Jesus, I give you everything that will happen this week. I entrust to you my spouse, my children, and every moment that awaits us: the blessings and the trials. This week begins and ends with you, the Alpha and the Omega. Jesus, I Trust in You." In that moment, even as the week ahead stretches before me, I remember that holiness is not out of reach. It is for every family, right in the middle of the chaos, the laughter, the rush, and even the moments that feel unsure.

Families today face many challenges: busyness, uncertainty, and the constant pressures of a world that often drifts far from God. Yet amid these trials, the Church never ceases to proclaim a truth that brings hope. The family remains at the very heart of God's plan for humanity. The first American Augustinian pontiff, Pope Leo XIV, reminded the Church in one of his earliest addresses that families, when grounded in Christ's love, become a sign of peace for the world. "Families are the cradle of the future of humanity," he said. These words echo the Church's constant teaching and offer us encouragement as we begin this consecration.

This thirty-three-day journey is not about achieving perfection but about opening our hearts and homes more fully to the love of Jesus, Mary, and Joseph. By consecrating ourselves to Jesus through the Holy Family, we invite their presence into our joys and sorrows, our work and rest, our ordinary routines and extraordinary moments.

The following thirty-three days are structured as a spiritual journey with the Holy Family. Each day begins with a line from the Litany of the Holy Family, which serves as a guidepost for prayer. That line draws our attention to a particular truth or mystery in the lives of Jesus, Mary, and Joseph. Alongside it, you will find Scripture, meditation, reflection questions, and prayer. All are tools that invite you to weave the example of the Holy Family into the very fabric of your life.

Step by step, day by day, these reflections lead us deeper into the spirit of Nazareth, where love, humility, and fidelity to God quietly transformed an ordinary household into the heart of salvation history.

As you begin this journey, trust that the Holy Family walks beside you. Joseph will guide you with courage, Mary with tenderness, and Jesus with His merciful Heart. Together, they show us how ordinary family life, lived with love, becomes extraordinary in God's eyes.

# 33-DAYS TO NAZARETH JOY

A Consecration to Jesus Through the Holy Family

# Litany of the Holy Family

Lord, have mercy.
Christ, have mercy.
Lord, have mercy.
Christ, hear us.
Christ, graciously hear us.
God, the Father of Heaven, have mercy on us.
God the Son, Redeemer of the world, have mercy on us.
God, the Holy Spirit, have mercy on us.
Holy Trinity, one God, have mercy on us.

*("Pray for us" is repeated as indicated by "...")*

Jesus, Mary, and Joseph, ...
Jesus, Mary, and Joseph, most worthy of our veneration, ...
Jesus, Mary, and Joseph, called "the Holy Family" from all time, ...

Jesus, Mary, and Joseph, son, mother, and head of the Holy Family, . . .

Jesus, Mary, and Joseph, divine child, pure spouse, and chaste spouse, . . .

Jesus, Mary, and Joseph, restorers of fallen families, . . .

Jesus, Mary, and Joseph, image of the Blessed Trinity here on earth, . . .

Holy Family, tested by the greatest of difficulties, . . .

Holy Family, with much suffering on the journey to Bethlehem, . . .

Holy Family, without a welcome in Bethlehem, . . .

Holy Family, visited by the poor shepherds, . . .

Holy Family, obliged to live in a stable, . . .

Holy Family, praised by the angels, . . .

Holy Family, venerated by the wise men from the East, . . .

Holy Family, greeted by the pious Simeon in the temple, . . .

Holy Family, persecuted and exiled to a foreign country, . . .

Holy Family, hidden and unknown in Nazareth, . . .

Holy Family, faithful in the observance of
   divine laws, . . .
Holy Family, perfect model of the Christian
   family, . . .
Holy Family, center of peace and concord, . . .
Holy Family, whose protector is a model of
   paternal care, . . .
Holy Family, whose mother is a model of
   maternal diligence, . . .
Holy Family, whose Divine Child is a model of
   filial obedience, . . .
Holy Family, poor in material goods, but rich
   in divine blessings, . . .
Holy Family, as nothing in the eyes of men, but
   so great in heaven, . . .
Holy Family, our support in life and our hope
   in death, . . .
Holy Family, patron and protector of our
   family, . . .
Jesus, Mary, and Joseph, pray for us.
Lamb of God, who takes away the sins of the
   world, spare us, O Lord.
Lamb of God, who takes away the sins of the
   world, hear us, O Lord.

Lamb of God, who takes away the sins of the world, have mercy on us.
Christ, hear us.
Christ, graciously hear us.
Let us pray. O God of infinite goodness and kindness, who has deigned to call us to this family,
Give us the grace to venerate Jesus, Mary, and Joseph, so that, imitating them in this life, we may enjoy with them the life to come.
We ask this through Christ Our Lord.
Amen.

# Introduction

To consecrate means to set apart for God. When we consecrate ourselves, we are offering our lives, our homes, and our families entirely to Him. Consecration is a private devotional act that disposes our hearts to receive God's grace more fruitfully through participation in the Church's sacramental life. It is a simple yes, like Mary's *fiat*: a willing surrender that allows God to shape us into what He desires us to be.

The Church has long recognized the power of consecrations to Jesus, to Mary, and to St. Joseph. Each consecration deepens our trust in God by uniting us with those who most closely reflect His love. There is a special grace for families who consecrate themselves to the Holy Family of Nazareth.

Why the Holy Family? Because Nazareth is where holiness entered the daily routines of family life. Jesus grew up under the watchful care of Joseph and the tender love of Mary. Their home was filled not with wealth or status, but with prayer, trust, work, and love. The Holy Family teaches us that holiness is possible in every home, regardless of how tested by trials or how simple.

This book will guide you on a 33-day journey of preparation through the Litany of the Holy Family. Each day's line from the litany opens a window into the mysteries, virtues, and everyday life of Jesus, Mary, and Joseph, inviting you to draw closer to them in prayer and reflection.

Each day concludes with reflection questions and a short prayer to help you apply the teaching personally and within your home. On Day 34, you will pray the Act of Consecration to the Holy Family, bringing this journey to fulfillment by entrusting your family to their patronage and protection.

This is not a test of perfection. It is an invitation to walk alongside Jesus, Mary, and Joseph. In doing so, they will guide you in learning from their example, allowing God to forge your family in virtue, and discovering joy in living together as a family.

May Pope Leo XIV's words resound in your heart as you begin: "In the family, faith is handed on together with life, generation after generation. It is shared like food at the family table and like the love in our hearts. In this way, families become privileged places in which to encounter Jesus, who loves us and desires our good, always." May your consecration strengthen your family to become a sign of love and a witness of God's mercy and hope for the Church and for the world.

# How to Use this Book

This 33-day consecration is meant to be simple and doable for every family. Whether you are parents or grandparents, guardians, engaged couples, spouses, single adults, or children, this journey is designed to help you open your home and heart more fully to Jesus through his Holy Family.

## Daily Structure

1. **Invocation:** A line from the Litany of the Holy Family.
2. **Scripture Reading:** A passage of God's Word to frame the day.
3. **Meditation:** A reflection that draws out the meaning of our lives.

4. **Family Application:** Simple practices or suggestions to live the lesson in daily life.
5. **Closing Prayer:** Entrusting the day to God in the presence of Jesus, Mary, and Joseph.
6. **Reflection Questions:** Prompts for personal or family conversation and prayer

## Time of Day

Choose a time that works best for your family: morning, during the day, after dinner, or before bedtime.

- If your family's schedule is busy, read the Scripture and Meditation aloud, and keep the prayer short.
- If you are praying alone, take a few extra moments to journal your responses to the reflection questions.
- If you forget one day, or more than a few, don't give up. Come back to where you last left off. Try to catch up. God understands our busyness.

## Practical Tips

- **Make it visible:** Create a prayer corner with an image of the Holy Family.
- **Keep it short:** Children, especially, will engage best when the daily reflection is simple and prayerful.
- **Adapt as needed:** Some days, you may pray only the Scripture and Prayer; other days, you may include the full reflection and discussion.

## The Goal

This consecration is not about perfection, but about presence. By showing up each day with open hearts, you will invite the Holy Family into your home, little by little, until your family life becomes more reflective of Nazareth.

I saw this firsthand when we made our first consecration to Jesus through Mary. Simply gathering all of us in the same room each evening felt like a victory. It was hard to do, but somehow, by God's grace, we managed it. The journey itself had its ups and downs. We started strong, reading the book and prayers together every night that first week. Then life happened.

We fell off the bandwagon, often hitting awkward ruts in the road. We missed a day here, a couple more there, before climbing back on, catching up, and finishing strong.

What surprised us most as parents was the fruit we began to see over time: quiet during prayer, attentiveness, questions about the material, a growing interest in the faith, and more laughter around the table. It wasn't perfect, but the simple act of showing up day after day allowed grace to seep into the fabric of our family life in ways we never expected.

# Suggested Starting Dates

You may begin your 33-day preparation so that the day of consecration falls on one of the following feast days associated with Jesus, Mary, or Joseph. Below are examples of when to begin, with feast-day dates based on the General Roman Calendar (check each year's liturgical calendar for adjustments).

**Feast of the Holy Family**

- **Feast Date:** Sunday within the Octave of Christmas, usually the Sunday after Christmas
- **Start Date:** Late November or early December (varies each year)
- **Spiritual Focus:** Perfect for families consecrating together during Advent or Christmastide.

### Solemnity of St. Joseph, Spouse of the Blessed Virgin Mary

- **Solemnity Date:** March 19
- **Start Date:** February 15
- **Spiritual Focus:** Focuses on Joseph's obedience, protection, and paternal care.

### Feast of the Annunciation

- **Feast Date:** March 25
- **Start Date:** February 21
- **Spiritual Focus:** Centers on Mary's *fiat* and surrender to God's will.

### Feast of St. Joseph the Worker

- **Feast Date:** May 1
- **Start Date:** March 29
- **Spiritual Focus:** Emphasizes the sanctity of daily work and family life.

### Solemnity of the Immaculate Heart of Mary

- **Solemnity Date:** Saturday after the Solemnity of the Sacred Heart, mid-June
- **Start Date:** Mid-May (date varies)
- **Spiritual Focus:** Focuses on purity of heart and love of the Mother of God.

## Solemnity of the Sacred Heart of Jesus

- **Solemnity Date:** Friday after Corpus Christi, mid-June
- **Start Date:** Mid-May (date varies)
- **Spiritual Focus:** A consecration uniting the Holy Family devotion with the Heart of Jesus.

## Feast of the Nativity of the Blessed Virgin Mary

- **Feast Date:** September 8
- **Start Date:** August 6
- **Spiritual Focus:** Celebrates Mary's birth and role as Mother of the Holy Family.

## Feast of the Presentation of the Blessed Virgin Mary

- **Feast Date:** November 21
- **Start Date:** October 19
- **Spiritual Focus:** Ideal for those dedicating themselves before Advent begins.

## Christmas Day

- **Feast Date:** December 25
- **Start Date:** November 22
- **Spiritual Focus:** Beautiful for families wishing to consecrate during Christmas.

## Practical Tip for Families

If a feast date does not perfectly fit your calendar, choose any significant family date (a baptism anniversary, wedding anniversary, or a saint's feast meaningful to your home) as your consecration day. The important part is the spirit of preparation, not the calendar itself.

## How to Calculate Your Start Date

Each consecration follows a 33-day period of preparation, with the feast day itself as the 34th day, the day of consecration.

To determine your start date, simply count back 33 days from your chosen feast. Begin your daily prayers and reflections on that day so that your final act of consecration is made on the feast itself.

For example, if you wish to consecrate your family on the Solemnity of St. Joseph (March 19), you would begin the preparation on February 15.

You may also repeat this 33-day preparation each year as a spiritual renewal, allowing your family's consecration to deepen and grow over time.

## A Note for Families

This consecration is designed to serve families of every shape, size, and season. The beginning section offers background and spiritual foundations to deepen your understanding of consecration and family holiness. If your family is ready to begin praying right away, feel free to turn directly to the 33-Day Consecration to the Holy Family. You can always return to the first section later to read and reflect more deeply. The Holy Family meets us wherever we begin; what matters most is that we begin together.

PREPARING THE HEART

# Foundations of Consecration

# Foundations of Consecration

You are about to embark on the 33-Day Consecration to the Holy Family. This is a profound opportunity to draw closer to Jesus, Mary, and Joseph, who, as a family, are an ideal model of love, faith, and virtue. In their hidden life at Nazareth, they reveal how holiness is lived not in extraordinary deeds, but in the ordinary moments of family life. By journeying with them and dedicating yourself to this path, you will be invited to conform your own heart and home more fully to the life of Christ. You will also open yourself to the transformative power of God's grace, love, and mercy, discovering in the Holy Family both a refuge of peace and a school of discipleship.

This consecration is an adventure of the heart, one that I trust will overflow with God's good surprises. It will help you both personally and collectively by encouraging you to grow in holiness through the trials and triumphs of life.

By God's grace, the seeds planted through this consecration will bear the fruit of peace and healing in your family. If you enter with an open heart, you will become more receptive to God's grace, allowing it to work more tangibly in your life.

Through this consecration, your household will also learn to cultivate virtues that are essential for living a holy life: humility, patience, obedience, and self-giving love. The Holy Family, united in their unwavering trust in God, demonstrates how to live out these virtues even amid trials.

God's grace has completely transformed my own family through Mary and St. Joseph and the Consecrations to Jesus. I have witnessed each of us, most especially the children, emerge with a deeper relationship with Christ and a newfound joy in Mary and Joseph as true heavenly friends and powerful intercessors. When we first prayed a consecration as a family, our children were very young. We weren't sure how much they understood, but I will never forget the satisfaction on their faces when we finished. They seemed deeply content, as if they knew something important had been completed. They shared in our hope that our deepest prayers and desires might soon be answered. To me, that moment showed we had planted a tiny mustard seed of hope. It serves as a reminder that consecrations lay down roots of hunger for God, even in young hearts.

May you, too, discover in this journey not only the blessing of consecration, but also a hunger for what lies beyond it: a desire to remain always close to the Holy Family. As you enter into the hidden life of Jesus, Mary, and Joseph in Nazareth, may God reveal how your own family life can be sanctified, filling your daily routines and relationships with his presence.

## What Is Consecration?

Before beginning the Consecration to the Holy Family, let's take a moment to ponder what this word means.

At its core, to consecrate means to set oneself apart for a sacred purpose. "Consecration" comes from the Latin verb *consecrāre*, which suggests the idea of making something entirely holy or fully dedicated to God. Consecration also signifies a change from the "old" to the "new." It echoes the words of St. Paul as he exhorts the Colossians to "put off the old self with its practices" and "to put on the new self which is being renewed in knowledge after the image of its creator" (Colossians 3:9-10). This is why each consecration is not just a devotion, but an invitation to real conversion. Before and during the consecration, we can ask God for the grace to be radically changed in a particular area of our lives, to put aside a specific sin or vice, and to grow in virtue.

In our own family, we often approach a consecration by naming one area where we most need God's help. Sometimes it is a tendency toward impatience; other times it is the temptation to speak harshly instead of gently. Each time, we bring that weakness honestly before God and ask for the grace to be changed. I have seen how powerful this can be. What feels like an unshakable habit begins to soften under God's mercy, and little by little, growth becomes possible. For us, this practice has made consecration not only an act of devotion, but a concrete step toward holiness.

One example stands out vividly. For quite some time, I noticed one of our older children growing increasingly impatient with a younger sibling. Before beginning our consecration, I pulled this child aside and asked if they would consider praying about their impatience, since it was affecting the peace of our home. The younger sibling was not trying to cause trouble; they simply wanted to be near their older brother or sister, exploring toys, peeking into their room, or tagging along. I reminded the older one, "This is really a compliment. They want to be like you." To my surprise, the older sibling agreed to bring this into the consecration.

At first, I thought real change would be impossible. Yet slowly, sometimes only in drips, the impatience softened. Now, instead of reacting defensively, the older sibling often invites the little one to share in their treasures and secrets. At times, I catch them spontaneously hugging; it always makes me smile. It became a small but powerful reminder that consecration opens the door for God's grace to transform even the hardest places in family life.

## To Jesus Through His Family

Within Catholic Tradition, personal consecrations hold a privileged place in deepening the faithful's relationship with Jesus Christ. Among the most renowned and influential forms of consecration is the "Total Consecration to Jesus through Mary," popularized by St. Louis-Marie Grignion de Montfort, the 17th-century Third Order Dominican priest. This devotion highlights a relationship with the Blessed Virgin Mary as the "quickest, surest, and easiest" path to an intimate union with her son, Jesus.

Devotion to the Holy Family has gained renewed attention in Catholic life. Montfort's Marian consecration found a solid place in Catholic devotional life, and a complementary devotion to St. Joseph also opened the way to this new 33-day Consecration to the Holy Family. This consecration to Jesus, Mary, and Joseph emphasizes the virtues of family life, as modeled at Nazareth, and invites those wanting to grow in holiness in a practical and achievable way.

## This Consecration Is for Everyone

When we think of the Holy Family, we often imagine an idyllic scene in Nazareth: a sinless child with a perfect mother and saintly father in a home filled with peace. It can feel almost unreachable. How could we, with our imperfect families, ever hope to reflect such holiness?

The truth is, even the Holy Family endured hardships. They faced poverty in Bethlehem, rejection from their neighbors, and the danger of King Herod's wrath that forced them to flee into Egypt. Their home was not free from fear, uncertainty, or sacrifice. What we see in Nazareth is only one snapshot of their lives. Their holiness was not born from ease or comfort but from trusting God during trials, and most of all, God's grace. It is precisely there that we can find encouragement for our own families.

As you begin this consecration, remember that God does not ask you to start from perfection. He meets you where you are: within your struggles, weaknesses, and deepest needs. Jesus himself said, "I came not to call the righteous, but sinners"

(Matthew 9:13). That means this consecration is especially for us who fall short. It is for all of us. As St. Paul reminds us, "All have sinned and fall short of the glory of God" (Romans 3:23).

No matter your state in life, this journey into the heart of the Holy Family is meant for you. It is not only about personal renewal but also about the sanctification of the family, and, through it, the wider Body of Christ. Even those who have drifted from the Faith are not excluded; God's mercy always invites them home.

## Saying "Yes" to the Christ Who Knocks

Have you ever seen the well-known painting of Jesus standing at the door, knocking? If you look closely, the doorknob rests on the inside of the door. There is no way for Jesus to open the door of our hearts unless we open it from within. If you open the door, the Lord will come in and dine with you in a personal and intimate way. Our Lord says to us all, "Behold, I stand at the door and knock. If anyone hears my voice and opens the door, [then] I will enter his house and dine with him, and he with me" (Revelation 3:20).

This image has always been deeply personal for me. When I was a child, I had a beautiful print of this painting hanging on the wall of my bedroom. Each night before I fell asleep, I would look at Jesus knocking and whisper goodnight to him. Though I didn't understand it then, the picture held a quiet mystery that stayed with me into adulthood. Only later did I realize the deeper truth: that the doorknob was missing on the outside because it rests on the inside. Jesus was waiting patiently for me, as he waits for each of us, to freely choose to open the door of our hearts to Him.

Let's open the doors of our hearts! Let's pursue the way of holiness that the humble home of Nazareth fostered within its walls. May your family be abundantly blessed by the Holy Family of Jesus, Mary, and Joseph. May their example of love, faith, and holiness guide you as you strive to grow in virtue and sanctity, imitating the sacred bond that sanctified family life in the humble home of Nazareth.

# Marian and Holy Family Consecration

St. Louis de Montfort is celebrated for his profound Marian spirituality, especially outlined in his classic treatise, *True Devotion to Mary*. While his writings place strong emphasis on the Blessed Virgin, Montfort's ultimate goal is Christ-centered. He highlights that Mary is the most direct route to Jesus because she is his mother, the one who carried him in her womb, nurtured him throughout his earthly life, and always remains perfectly united to his divine will.

Montfort draws from biblical imagery, including passages like Luke 1:38, where Mary responds with her *fiat*: "Behold, I am the handmaid of the Lord; let it be to me according to your word." This act of unwavering faith is seen as the apex of humble obedience, making Mary the "perfect disciple" and thus the perfect intermediary to lead us to Jesus.

Within Montfort's spirituality, the concept of "Marian mediation" does not detract from Christ's unique role as the one Mediator between God and man (1 Timothy 2:5). Rather, Mary's mediation is wholly dependent on Christ's mediatorship, serving as a subordinate participation in His grace, an echo of how God chose to bring the Redeemer into the world through her (Luke 1:30–33).

The hallmark of Montfort's practice, as he explains, is the believer's total gift of self to Mary: body, soul, goods, merits, and intentions. The logic is simple yet profound. If we give ourselves entirely to Mary, she will purify and safeguard our offerings, presenting them more perfectly to her son. Thus, the faithful become more fully "belonging to Jesus through Mary" and strengthened in their baptismal vows. While Montfort's approach may appear "Marian" on its face, it is entirely oriented toward uniting the soul with Christ. Mary is not the end, but the most effective means to that end.

I saw this truth in a small way when we first began teaching our children to pray the Rosary. At first, it was just the two of us as parents praying aloud while the kids listened. Soon they began joining in with the second half of the Hail Mary, and before long, one of them was leading an entire decade. The Rosary became something we could pray together as a family.

Does it happen every night? Not always, but it remains one of our greatest goals. What I have noticed, though, is that on the nights when we do pray together, there is a greater peace in our home. We are gentler with one another, more patient, and the day's challenges do not weigh as heavily. I especially loved the way my husband explained going to Jesus through Mary to our children, and I could see it resonated with them. He said, "You know how, when you really want something, you sometimes go to Mom first, knowing she'll speak to me and explain why it matters? That's how Mary is with Jesus. When we pray the Rosary, we go to his mother, the soft place in his heart, and he is more likely to say yes to her request."

The simple rhythm of the Rosary reminds us that consecration works in the same way. Just as at the wedding feast at Cana, where Jesus responded to Mary's prompting (John 2:1–11), we, too, learn to lean on her intercession. And like children learning to walk, sometimes faltering, sometimes stumbling, our small, faithful steps in prayer draw us closer to the heart of her son.

When I first heard of St. Louis de Montfort's consecration to Mary, it felt overwhelming, and for years, I put it off. There were so many prayers, and I could never seem to keep track of them all. I would lose my place, worry that I wasn't doing it perfectly, and eventually stop midway. Deep down, I also felt unworthy. I felt hesitant to approach Mary in prayer because I was not sure I could live up to what God might be asking of me. Looking back, I see that I had missed the heart of consecration. God does not ask for perfection; he asks for trust. And Mary, as a gentle mother, does not push us away for our weakness but tenderly draws us close to her son.

It was only when I began to learn these two lessons (that Jesus loves us where we are, and that Mary's presence is marked by gentleness) that I finally approached the consecration with greater confidence. Eventually, my spouse and I prayed it together from beginning to end, and through it, I discovered a closeness to Christ I had not expected. Mary revealed herself as a true mother, guiding me by the hand to her son. Later, when we consecrated our family to St. Joseph, I experienced the steadying presence of a father who never ceases to hear us and faithfully obtains answers to prayer.

## What Is a Total Consecration to the Holy Family?

A "Total Consecration to the Holy Family" widens the lens from Mary to the whole context of the Holy Family of Nazareth: Jesus, Mary, and Joseph. Each of these three holy persons holds a unique role in salvation history.

- **Jesus:** He is the Incarnate Son of God, the Second Person of the Trinity made flesh. He is our Redeemer and the definitive center of all devotion.
- **Mary:** She is the Mother of God (*Theotokos*), the New Eve, and the perfect disciple. Her "yes" (*fiat*) opened the way for the Incarnation, and she remains intimately united with her son in his saving mission.
- **Joseph:** As the foster father of Jesus and the chaste spouse of Mary, he is the "Guardian of the Redeemer." Scripture calls him a "just man" (Matthew 1:19) who exemplifies obedience, humility, and paternal protectiveness.

A Holy Family Consecration acknowledges the earthly "trinity" of Nazareth: an image of unity and cooperation in God's plan. Rather than focusing solely on Mary's mediation, this consecration integrates Joseph's paternal example and fatherly intercession and keeps Jesus at the center.

## Emphasis on the Virtues of Family Life

One of the strongest appeals of a Holy Family Consecration is its invitation to emulate the family virtues that characterized life in Nazareth. These virtues include the following:

1. **Humility:** The Incarnate Word chose to dwell in a simple home, far from riches or earthly grandeur.
2. **Obedience:** Jesus was obedient to Mary and Joseph (Luke 2:51), Mary was obedient to God's will (Luke 1:38), and Joseph was obedient to the divine instructions given in dreams. First, when the angel told him not to be afraid to take Mary as his wife (Matthew 1:20–21), and later, when the angel warned him to flee with his family to Egypt (Matthew 2:13).
3. **Charity:** Their household was a living school of love, where self-giving was the norm.
4. **Purity:** Mary's and Joseph's virginal union highlights chastity of body and purity of heart.
5. **Unity:** The Holy Family remained one in purpose and mission, united around Christ.

By consecrating oneself to the Holy Family, we strive to take in these virtues and carry them into daily life, regardless of one's path.

## A Communal, Familial Dimension

While Montfort's teaching focuses strongly on Mary's maternal mediation, a Holy Family Consecration adds a more pronounced communal or familial dynamic. Joseph's paternal role can resonate deeply with fathers and husbands, while Mary's maternal role can speak to mothers and wives. Children learn from the Child Jesus, who "grew and became strong" (Luke 2:40), modeling obedience and virtue.

Even when modern family dynamics differ from the traditional roles exemplified in Nazareth, each family member can still identify personally with Jesus, Mary, and Joseph. Mothers and fathers, grandparents and guardians, single parents and working parents can find inspiration and encouragement in the virtues of the Holy Family.

Ultimately, what unites families to Nazareth is not external structure, but the love, fidelity, and mutual care modeled by Jesus, Mary, and Joseph. In essence, families who pray together in consecration to the Holy Family begin to see themselves as participating in the life and example of Nazareth's holy household.

# How All Consecrations Lead to Jesus

Regardless of whether one follows Montfort's Marian perspective, a St. Joseph lens, or a Holy Family approach, Christ remains the ultimate focal point:

- **Marian Consecration:** Mary is presented as the surest path to Jesus. She always says, "Do whatever He tells you" (John 2:5).
- **St. Joseph Consecration:** Joseph's consecration invites individuals and families to place themselves under his guidance and intercession, aiming to imitate his virtues and deepen their relationship with Jesus Christ.
- **Holy Family Consecration:** Jesus is openly acknowledged as the divine Son and the "end" of all devotion, with Mary and Joseph offering complementary paths of maternal and paternal guidance.

In each case, Mary and Joseph are not the end, but guides pointing to Christ at the heart of all the devotions.

# Entering the Hidden Life of Nazareth

Since the earliest days of Christianity, believers have looked to the Holy Family as a vivid example of sanctity lived out in the routine of daily life. This ideal finds its deepest expression in the "hidden years" of Christ at Nazareth (Luke 2:51–52). In these, Scripture offers only brief glimpses of the Lord's upbringing. Though outwardly hidden, these years remain a rich treasury for meditation and devotion.

Pope St. Paul VI called Nazareth the "school of the Gospel," teaching us that the ordinary rhythms of family life can become a profound path to holiness. During his 1964 visit to the Basilica of the Annunciation, he reflected on how the Holy Family embodied a spirit of silence and interiority (Reflections at Nazareth, §2). In that silence, Mary pondered the mysteries of her son, Joseph discerned God's direction in dreams, and Jesus grew in wisdom and grace before both God and neighbor.

In our noisy and distracted world, this lesson is more relevant than ever. The Holy Family shows us that holiness is not achieved only through extraordinary deeds, but through love for God, family, and neighbor. Their witness calls us to create moments of quiet reflection, to listen for God's voice amid ordinary responsibilities, and to allow our homes, however imperfect, to become schools of prayer, charity, and virtue.

Nazareth was sacred precisely because it was humble. It was there that Jesus learned obedience in the daily tasks of family life by working beside Joseph, helping Mary with household duties, and praying within the cadence of their home. This hidden yet profoundly holy existence reminds us that our waking, working, and resting (down to the smallest tasks) can be sanctified when performed faithfully and with love.

St. Thérèse of Lisieux, known as the Little Flower, taught in her autobiography, *Story of a Soul*, that holiness is found in small, hidden acts of love and trust in God. She called this the "Little Way," which is discovering holiness in acts of sacrifice and love unseen by the world. St. Teresa of Calcutta, the saint of the poor, captured the same truth when she wrote in *A Simple Path*: "Wash the plate not because it is dirty but because you love the person who will use it next."

The littleness of Nazareth shows us that holiness is found in the ordinary: putting groceries away, saying grace before meals, forgiving quickly after an argument, helping a sick family member, or listening patiently to one another. Each small act, done in love, becomes an offering to God. In this way, the home becomes a workshop of grace. By embracing the littleness of ordinary life, families mirror the holiness of Nazareth and allow Christ to transform the routine into the sacred.

One evening, I caught a glimpse of this truth in the middle of an ordinary chore. I was frustrated by the teetering pile of dishes waiting in the sink. As I began rinsing them before placing them in the dishwasher, one of my children wandered in, started taking dishes from me, and slid them into the machine. Then my husband joined in, clearing the plates from the table that were hard for me to reach. Soon, we had become an assembly line. We all worked side by side while another sibling babysat the youngest. In that small, ordinary moment, my heart softened. The dishes weren't just dishes anymore. They became a little act of love, a hidden way of caring for one another and serving Christ. It reminded me that Nazareth is not far away; it is found right here, in the unnoticed corners of daily family life.

Nazareth continues to teach us that:

- Every home can become a sanctuary when Christ is at its center.
- Every act of service can be transformed into an offering of love.
- Every family member has a role in reflecting the virtues of Jesus, Mary, and Joseph.

By contemplating the hidden life of the Holy Family, we discover how prayer, labor, and silence, practiced in love, turn the ordinary into the extraordinary. In this sense, a Consecration to the Holy Family is more than a devotion. It is an invitation to live daily life in union with the Gospel, aligning our homes and hearts with the grace of Nazareth.

## Universal Call to Holiness

This vision of family life, rooted in God's plan from the beginning, was reaffirmed in the teaching of the Second Vatican Council. In *Lumen Gentium*, the Council reminds us that all Christians, regardless of their state in life, share in the "universal call to holiness" (LG, 39–42). This means that the sanctity of family life is not confined to extraordinary achievements but is lived out through fidelity, sacrifice, and love in ordinary moments. The Holy Family uniquely exemplifies this Trinitarian paradigm: Jesus, Mary, and Joseph, each with their distinct roles and gifts, worked together in perfect harmony to fulfill God's salvific plan. Their daily interactions, grounded in trust, humility, obedience, and mutual respect, vividly illustrate the sanctity possible in ordinary family life.

This call is not abstract. It becomes concrete in the daily lives of families today. This truth became personal when my husband and I became parents for the first time. We came to realize in a tangible way that our marriage literally bore fruit in our children. In them, we saw how our love had become life-giving and outward-looking, a living reflection of the creative love of the Trinity. Yet even as we experienced this blessing, we came to understand that the call to holiness within the family is not dependent on the presence of children. Couples without children, as well as those who are single or consecrated, also participate in this Trinitarian love by faithfully offering themselves in service to God and others. Every family is called to reflect the communion of the Trinity.

In the Holy Family, we see the fullest expression of this truth lived out. The spousal life of Mary and Joseph shows how an "ordinary" life was transformed by the presence of Christ at Nazareth. When you consecrate yourselves to the Holy Family, your household enters that sacred dwelling spiritually. There, you embrace the simplicity, joy, and sanctity exemplified by Jesus, Mary, and Joseph.

When Christ is at the center, ordinary moments become sacred encounters. A family meal, for example, can echo the breaking of the bread. I often look at us all sitting around the table and imagine Jesus, Mary, and Joseph sharing a meal: food and drink, laughter, stories from their day, their hopes, challenges, and joys. Around our own table, we glimpse the mystery of self-giving love. Each person offers themselves in their presence, stories, and love, as a gift to the other.

The simple acts of serving one another (such as passing bread, pouring water, and listening with care) become reflections of Christ's love. In this way, the table becomes more than a place of eating; it becomes a place of communion, where love is shared and Christ is present. Every family table, when Christ is welcomed, becomes a little Nazareth.

## Prayer, Labor, and Silence in the Holy Family

A hallmark of the Holy Family's life is their harmonious rhythm of prayer, labor, and silence. This balance was exemplified particularly vividly by St. Joseph, but also unmistakably reflected in the lives of Mary and Jesus. Scripture offers us profound insights into this sacred harmony.

## Prayer

As mentioned previously, St. Joseph exemplifies a life of prayer through his attentive listening and obedience to divine guidance received through dreams (Matthew 1:19–20; 2:13–14).

Similarly, Mary embodies contemplative prayer, quietly pondering divine mysteries in her heart (Luke 2:19, 2:51). Her interior relationship with God allowed her to embrace with trust and patience both joys and sorrows.

In this prayer-rich atmosphere, we can envision the young Jesus joining his parents daily in reciting traditional Jewish prayers and Psalms. Indeed, the depth of Jesus' later ministry reveals that he had the Psalms and Scriptures memorized, words he had prayed and absorbed since childhood in Nazareth. Their shared prayer life flourished because it was rooted in mutual love for God and for one another.

In our own home, family prayer has never been picture-perfect. When the children were younger, the Rosary often meant fidgeting, yawning, or wandering attention. But over time, I noticed something remarkable. Even in the chaos, peace slowly settled in. By the end of prayer, the tension of the day often lifted, and the room felt calmer. It taught me that prayer in family life doesn't need to be polished to be powerful; God meets us even in the imperfect offerings.

## Labor

Joseph's diligent labor as a *tekton*, often translated as carpenter or craftsman, beautifully demonstrates the sacred dignity inherent in daily work. This honorable vocation provided for his family's material needs and instilled in Jesus the value and dignity of honest labor. This is evidenced when his neighbors identified him as "the carpenter's son" (Matthew 13:55). The Church underscores this sacredness of labor, teaching that honest human work, done faithfully and with love, participates intimately in God's ongoing creative act (Laborem Exercens, St. John Paul II).

Yet Joseph was not alone in sanctifying the home through labor. Mary, too, transformed everyday tasks such as cooking, cleaning, and managing household resources into spiritual offerings by performing them with love and faithfulness. Likewise, Jesus learned the carpenter's trade from Joseph, experiencing firsthand how diligent labor could glorify God. Families today can emulate the Holy Family's example by viewing daily chores, employment, and study as opportunities to serve God and one another, transforming their homes into genuine Nazareths.

I recall times when our children resisted doing chores, especially when it came to cleaning up their toys or helping with the dishes. At first, it felt like an endless battle. But as we encouraged them to see these small tasks as ways of serving one another, something began to change.

Slowly, the grumbling gave way to teamwork, and even laughter at times. These ordinary chores became moments of hidden love. They transformed into simple offerings that united us more closely as a family and, in their own way, united us with God.

## Silence

Silence, the third pillar of Nazareth's sanctity, is exemplified powerfully by Joseph's quiet presence. His silence was not passive; it was active and attentive. He demonstrated a deliberate posture of listening and readiness to act on God's word. In a contemporary world saturated with noise, Joseph's fidelity calls modern families to carve out spaces of quiet discernment, enabling them to hear God's voice and to respond courageously.

Mary likewise demonstrates the power of reflective silence. When facing uncertainties, such as the distress of losing Jesus in Jerusalem (Luke 2:41–51), her response was not frantic questioning but quiet trust in God's providence. Formed in this atmosphere, Jesus himself lived the fruit of silence. He stood silent before his accusers (Matthew 26:63) and frequently sought solitude to commune deeply with the Father (Luke 5:16).

Silence can feel especially difficult in the context of modern family life, where noise, activity, and constant distraction often fill our homes. Yet even in these circumstances, choosing silence becomes a way of making space for God's voice. In our own family, silence is not easy. With children in the house, there is always conversation, laughter, or squabbling, and I sometimes imagine that if I were on retreat, silence would come naturally. But because it doesn't, we have chosen to make it intentional. One small way we practice this is by turning off screens after dinner and spending time in quiet activities like prayer, journaling, or simply reading together. At first, it felt like an uphill battle, but over time, I have noticed how the stillness opens room in our hearts. It reminds me of the words of Scripture: "Be still, and know that I am God" (Psalm 46:10). These moments of chosen silence have become opportunities to listen for the Spirit's "still small voice" (1 Kings 19:12) amid the busyness of family life.

## Integrating the Examples of Joseph, Mary, and Jesus

Reflecting holistically on the Holy Family, we recognize how each member uniquely exemplifies prayer, labor, and silence:

- Joseph offers quiet obedience, diligent labor, and attentive silence, modeling how fathers can lead through humble yet firm faith.
- Mary exemplifies constant prayerful contemplation, faithful execution of daily tasks, and serene silence in the face of uncertainty, modeling for mothers (and indeed all Christians) the sanctity possible in ordinary living.
- Jesus, formed profoundly by Joseph and Mary's example, perfectly integrates these virtues throughout his earthly life, demonstrating how genuine holiness grows through consistent, daily fidelity to God's will.

Together, their lives show us how to transform our own families into domestic churches by becoming vibrant communities of prayer, sanctifying labor, and practicing reflective silence.

# The Family as the Domestic Church

Catholic teaching emphasizes that the family is more than a social unit; it is a living reflection of the Church. The family is a "domestic church," where holiness is cultivated and faith is passed on, becoming a vital source of witness and renewal for the world. The Second Vatican Council, in its document *Lumen Gentium*, referred to the family as the *ecclesia domestica* (LG, 11).

Later, Pope St. John Paul II expanded on this concept, stating: "The Christian family constitutes a specific revelation and realization of ecclesial communion, and for this reason, it can and should be called a 'domestic church'" (Familiaris Consortio, 21).

This concept is rooted in Scripture, where we see households like that of Priscilla and Aquila (Acts 18:2–3, 18, 26; Rom 16:3–5) serving as centers of prayer, fellowship, and hospitality. Thus, from the earliest days of the Church, families have been little "cells" of faith in which the Gospel is lived and proclaimed (CCC, 2207).

## Formation Ground of Faith

The home is holy ground. Yet we know that it does not always feel this way. No family is perfect. Our homes can be places of tension, misunderstanding, or division, where holiness seems hidden beneath the noise of daily life. But this is precisely where God chooses to dwell.

Holiness is not about being perfect. Christ calls us to "be perfect, as your heavenly Father is perfect" (Matthew 5:48), but this is not done without God's help. As parents, we often tell our children simply to "try their best." That is what God asks of us. Holiness begins here, in the daily effort to love. The family becomes the first school of virtue, where each member learns both self-gift and the humility of receiving from others. In this way, the home is both holy ground and a reflection of God's own life and love.

According to the Catechism of the Catholic Church: "The Christian family is a communion of persons, a sign and image of the communion of the Father and the Son in the Holy Spirit. In the procreation and education of children it reflects the Father's work of creation. It is called to partake of the prayer and sacrifice of Christ. Daily prayer and the reading of the Word of

God strengthen it in charity. The Christian family has an evangelizing and missionary task" (CCC, 2205).

This foundational aspect affirms that every member of the family becomes a participant in the Church's mission. As the living Church at home, our families shine with God's love in prayer and worship. We also reflect his love in the ordinary ways we care for one another, such as by sharing meals, practicing forgiveness, and putting others' needs before our own.

The home is often the very first place where children encounter the love of Christ. It is shared in the tender love of parents, guardians, and extended family members. In this environment, the seeds of faith can be planted and nurtured through everyday moments: blessings before meals, bedtime prayers, small acts of charity, and conversations about God's presence in daily life.

Some of my favorite moments are the simple ones. I love those unplanned times when my spouse or one of my children pulls me aside to share what's on their heart. Sometimes these moments are filled with words, and sometimes they are wrapped in silence. My favorite times with my husband are often when we are simply in each other's presence without needing to say anything at all. It is a silence that doesn't feel empty, but full, a silence that steadies the heart.

The spontaneous conversations are often filled with such grace. Sometimes it's a funny story that makes us laugh, other times it's a frustration or worry, and often it's just a little glimpse of what makes them happy. These moments, frequently hidden from the outside world, are where the life of the "school of love" becomes most real: in carving out space to listen, to love, and to be present to one another.

I'll admit, though, being present does not always come easily to me. I find myself confessing again and again that I am not always the best listener. With homeschooling, housework, and projects pressing on my mind, I often feel interrupted when one of my family members stops me to talk. And yet they do it constantly because they love to talk, and especially to me. They tell me it's because I'm a good listener, though I often doubt it. Still, I've stopped to wonder if this isn't a small reflection of God's heart. Every moment of every day, people around the world turn to him in prayer. Some come with thanksgiving, others with heavy burdens, others just needing to be heard. And God listens: patiently, attentively, without rushing us aside. The psalmist captures this so beautifully: "Incline your ear, O Lord, and answer me, for I am poor and needy" (Psalm 86:1). Perhaps that is why we instinctively trust Him. We know He always has time to hear us.

In this, I glimpse something of Nazareth. I imagine Jesus speaking freely to Mary and Joseph, sharing the little things of his day, his joys and questions, and finding in them hearts ready to listen. The quiet attentiveness of love marked their home. That same spirit of listening, however imperfectly I practice it, is part of what makes our families holy. When we make space to hear one another, we echo the Holy Family and invite Christ's presence into our homes.

These intentional moments, done faithfully and lovingly, root all of us in a personal relationship with Christ and a sense of belonging to one another and his Church. In this way, the ordinary rhythms of family life become extraordinary opportunities for grace, drawing us closer to God and to each other.

## Parents as First Witnesses of Faith

Building upon this vision, the Church teaches that parents are the first heralds of the Gospel for their children. The Catechism underscores this: "Parents have the first responsibility for the education of their children" (CCC, 2223) in the faith, prayer, and all the virtues.

This responsibility is not abstract. It means modeling Christian life, teaching the truths of the faith, and guiding children in prayer. As Deuteronomy 6:7 reminds us, God's commandments are to be taught diligently and spoken of "when you sit in your house, and when you walk by the way, and when you lie down, and when you rise." Parents today are called to do the same: to weave faith into the daily fabric of life, so that their children may see, hear, and experience the love of Christ through them.

For our family, this witness has been most visible through the sacraments and the rhythms of Catholic prayer. Since our children were babies, we sought to normalize faith as part of our daily life, attending Mass together, making visits to the Blessed Sacrament, talking freely about Jesus, and weaving prayer naturally into our home. One of the greatest blessings for us has been setting aside a weekly holy hour in adoration as a family. In that quiet space before the Eucharistic Lord, each of us (parents and children alike) learns how to listen, rest, and be with Jesus, echoing his invitation: "Abide in me, and I in you" (John 15:4).

We also go to confession together on a weekly basis. For our family, this practice has become a way to "begin again," to let Christ wipe away our sins and restore peace to our hearts. It is humbling to line up as a family, each of us in need of God's mercy, and to walk out renewed.

Jesus' words remind us: "Let the little children come to me, and do not hinder them; for to such belongs the kingdom of heaven" (Matthew 19:14). In the confessional and before the Blessed Sacrament, our children have learned that Christ's mercy and love are not distant ideas, but a living reality that embraces them personally.

As Pope Pius XI expressed in his encyclical *Divini Illius Magistri*, the family holds directly from the Creator the mission, and therefore the right, to educate the offspring. This truth reminds us that parental authority in spiritual matters is not merely a cultural norm, but a divine mandate, rooted in natural law and elevated by grace. Parents, by God's design, are entrusted with forming their children not only for earthly life, but for eternal life with him.

## The Modern Family

When we picture the Holy Family, it is easy to imagine an idyllic scene of a mother, father, and child living peacefully in Nazareth. Yet this image can feel distant from the complexities of modern life, where many families face divorce, single parenthood, the death of a spouse, long-distance separation, or other difficult circumstances. Today, children are often raised not only by parents but also by grandparents, extended family, foster parents, or guardians.

Faced with these realities, we may wonder: How can I relate to the Holy Family if my family looks so different from theirs?

The truth is that the Holy Family's example speaks to every household. Their virtues of obedience to God, mutual love and respect, humility, and trust in divine providence are not bound to one family model but are universally relevant.

In fact, the Holy Family itself was far from "conventional" in its time. Mary conceived Jesus by the power of the Holy Spirit (Luke 1:35). Joseph wrestled with doubt and considered quietly divorcing Mary until reassured by a divine dream (Matthew 1:19–21). Not long after, they fled to Egypt as strangers in a new land, forced into exile by Herod's persecution. And at the heart of their home, Mary and Joseph were entrusted with raising the Son of God in human flesh, a responsibility beyond imagining.

These moments show us that the Holy Family was no stranger to struggle, uncertainty, or upheaval. What made them holy was not a life free from hardship but their unwavering response of love and trust in God amid every trial.

By looking at what truly makes the Holy Family "holy," we discover that sanctity is found not in appearances or family structure but in fidelity to God and growth in charity. Whether in a traditional nuclear family, a blended family, or a household shaped by unique circumstances, every Christian family can imitate Jesus, Mary, and Joseph and reflect God's love in their own way.

And so, no matter your circumstances, take heart. God's grace is not limited to perfect homes or perfect people. Holiness begins where you are, in the concrete details of your daily life, and the Holy Family walks with you as companions and intercessors on the journey.

## Creating a Holy Family Culture

The Holy Family's life was anything but "typical" for their time, yet their unwavering trust in God set an example that transcends every era. Today's families face different trials, but the path to holiness remains the same: prayer, the sacraments, mutual love, and service.

A holy family culture begins with prayer. Whether it is the Rosary, reading the Bible together, or offering spontaneous prayers of thanksgiving, regular prayer strengthens the family bond in Christ. In my own family, I have seen the power of prayer, especially the Rosary, bring peace when nothing else could. Many have heard the famous words of Father Patrick Peyton: "The family that prays together stays together." While we are far from perfect in keeping this practice every day, we do our best.

There have been times when bickering at the dinner table, unfinished homework, and the chaos of scattered lidless markers, half-built towers of building bricks, and glitter-covered unicorn crafts made the whole evening feel heavy in an instant. Other times, it was deeper: worry over a sick child, job stress, or family tension that seemed to hang in the air. Yet in those moments, when we finally gathered in the living room to pray the Rosary, something shifted. At first, the prayers began unevenly (one child mumbling, another fidgeting, another poking a sibling) but soon the steady rhythm of the Hail Marys brought calm. By the time we reached the final decades, voices had softened, the atmosphere had changed, and I could sense God's presence drawing us back together. There was peace. What began in frustration ended in stillness, with unity and even a quiet joy.

If prayer is the heartbeat of family life, then the sacraments are its lifeblood. Sunday Mass, regular Confession, and the celebration of sacramental milestones anchor the home in God's grace. Through these encounters with Christ, children learn (more by experience than by words) that faith is not confined to Sundays but is meant to shape every part of life.

I will never forget the days each of my children became children of God at baptism. Each moment was its own story of grace. One cried without ceasing until just minutes before the rite began. As a nervous first-time parent, I feared the baby might wail through the entire ceremony, but he grew perfectly still and didn't even flinch when the icy water was poured over his head. Another was baptized in a font with heated water, warm like a little bath, but she burst into tears the instant it touched her forehead, almost as if to protest the surprise. And then there was a baptism marked by humility: a simple light green onesie beneath the white garment provided by the parish, and a family arriving late enough that I wondered if the priest might cancel with Mass about to begin in forty minutes. Yet in the end, she was calm and quiet, not making a sound.

Each baptism carried its own imperfections, its own worries and surprises, but each was perfect in the only way that matters: the Holy Spirit descended, Christ claimed them as his own, and our family was drawn more deeply into God's love. These sacramental beginnings remind me that the sacraments do more than mark milestones. They sustain the culture of prayer in family life, rooting our imperfect homes in the perfect grace of God.

Finally, the family as a "workshop of grace" exists not only for its own good but for the good of others. Acts of hospitality, service to the poor, and participation in parish life radiate God's love beyond the walls of the home. I think of one Thanksgiving season when our parish hosted a fundraiser for families who were struggling. Because that cause is close to our hearts (we have known times of uncertainty ourselves), we wanted to contribute in a way our children could join in. So, the kids eagerly baked two dozen sugar cookies and decorated them on their own. They did this with such joy and pride that I couldn't bear to correct a single smudge.

The finished decorated cookie tray still makes me smile to remember it: one-eyed turkeys, snowmen that had melted into smudges, unicorn cookies cracked in half, ornaments with icing so thick they were undecipherable. And the best of all, a creepy turkey that could have been a rock or perhaps some unknown farm animal. Their creations were messy, imperfect, and absolutely full of love. And at the end of the day, every last cookie sold, even the cracked ones. It was a small act, but one that showed our children that love, when offered generously, has a way of multiplying beyond what we can see. In those small, joyful offerings, our family caught a glimpse of Nazareth itself, where love sanctified even the simplest of things.

## Support from the Wider Church Community

No family is meant to journey alone. While our culture often prizes independence and self-reliance, the Catholic vision of family life is deeply communal. As the saying goes, "it takes a village." In the Church, that "village" is the family, parish, wider faith community, and the communion of saints. Families are called not only to nurture holiness within their own walls but also to draw strength from one another.

Parishes and Catholic communities exist to support parents, grandparents, and guardians in their roles as caregivers. Participation in adult faith formation, marriage enrichment programs, Bible studies, men's and women's groups, youth ministry, and children's catechesis allows families to receive wisdom and fellowship from the wider Church. In turn, strong families build strong parishes, and strong parishes form a strong Church.

The saints also remind us that holiness is often cultivated in community and family life. St. Louis and St. Zélie Martin, the parents of St. Thérèse of Lisieux, were canonized together as a married couple. They raised a family where deep faith and love shaped all five of their daughters, who entered religious life. Saints Joachim and Anne, the grandparents of Jesus, show us the importance of passing on the faith from one generation to the next. And St. Monica, through her tireless prayers and steadfast example, became the instrument of grace that led her son, St. Augustine, from a life of wandering into one of the greatest conversions in Church history. Her witness shows parents today that even when children stray, no prayer is wasted, and God's grace can bring forth abundant fruit in his time.

As St. Augustine wrote in *De Trinitate*: "If you see charity, you see the Trinity" (VIII.8). Fostering a holy family culture means seeing Christ in each family member, loving them, and together reflecting the perfect love of Father, Son, and Holy Spirit. And just as families are supported by grace within the sacraments, so, too, are they supported by the larger family of the Church, reminding us that we never walk the path of holiness alone.

## Living the Call

As you see, the call to live as "little Nazareths" is not reserved for idealized family arrangements. It is a universal call rooted in baptismal identity and the reality of God's boundless grace. The mission for all families remains the same: to become a reflection of the Holy Family rooted in faith, hope, and charity.

In a world saturated with noise and uncertainty, the family can stand as a beacon of Christ's love, illuminating society through humble, daily acts of kindness and prayer. For me, this image of the family as a beacon comes alive in a personal way. My family and I live near the shore, and from the time they were very little, my children have loved spending hours at the beach. Days would be spent soaking up the sunshine, chasing waves, and discovering hidden treasures in the sand: sea glass, sand dollars, tiny crabs, and shells. Yet one of the most awe-inspiring sights we have witnessed is the lighthouse piercing through the darkness at night, its steady light shining across the horizon. No matter how dark the sea, that beam offers safety, direction, and hope.

So, too, is the vocation of the Christian family. Just as Jesus is the Light of the World (John 8:12), each household is called to reflect His light into the world. The perennial call includes guiding, protecting, and offering hope amid the storms and shadows of modern life. In our homes, through prayer, forgiveness, hospitality, and love, we shine a light that points beyond ourselves to Christ.

May Jesus, Mary, and Joseph guide every family on this sacred journey, that each household may embody the love and unity of the Trinity and serve as a sign of hope for the whole world. For as Pope St. John Paul II reminded us: "As the family goes, so goes the nation and so goes the whole world in which we live."

As you begin this consecration, remember that the next thirty-three days are meant to be a journey, not a test. Each day will guide you through one line of the Litany of the Holy Family, along with Scripture, a meditation, prayer, and reflection questions.

If you fall behind, don't be discouraged. Just as in family life, some days don't go as planned. What matters most is faithfulness. God understands our interruptions, and he rejoices when we return. Think of this consecration not as a race to finish, but as a daily opportunity to open your heart more deeply to the love of Jesus, Mary, and Joseph.

# Prayer Before the Consecration

Jesus, Mary, and Joseph,
open our hearts to the grace of this
consecration.
Jesus, pour out your mercy upon us;
Mary, guide us with your motherly care;
Joseph, strengthen us with your faithful
prayers.
Prepare our homes to be little Nazareths,
where love, humility, and trust in God may
flourish.
As we begin this journey of consecration,
make us ready to receive all that the Holy
Family desires to give.
Keep us steadfast in faith, joyful in hope,
and united in the love of Christ, who is the
heart of every family.
Amen.

WEEK 1

# The Call of Mercy

# DAY 1

# Mercy at the Heart of the Gospel

*Lord, have mercy. Christ, have mercy. Lord, have mercy.*

## Opening Scripture

"The steadfast love of the Lord never ceases, his mercies never come to an end; they are new every morning; great is your faithfulness." *(Lamentations 3:22–23)*

## God is Mercy

From the very beginning, God has revealed himself as merciful. When Adam and Eve sinned, God did not abandon them. When Israel cried out in slavery, God delivered them. Again and again,

Scripture shows us a Father who hears his children, forgives their failings, and restores them with love.

Mercy is not something God does on the side; mercy is who he is. As Pope St. John Paul II reflected, "Mercy is love's second name" (Dives in Misericordia, 7). Jesus is the visible face of that mercy. In him, the Father's compassion takes on flesh. Every healing, every act of forgiveness, every parable of Jesus shows us a God whose heart bends toward the broken and lost.

We all sin, as St. Paul reminds us: "All have sinned and fall short of the glory of God" (Romans 3:23). I often teach my children that mistakes are part of life, but they can also become stepping stones to sanctity. St. Thérèse of Lisieux once said that even our faults can help us grow closer to God when we return to him with humility. Everything, especially mistakes, can lead us closer to Christ.

In our home, I remind my kids that it is not the mistake itself that should define us, but how we respond afterward. Jesus says, "You, therefore, must be perfect, as your heavenly Father is perfect" (Matthew 5:48). While we strive toward holiness, sin is ultimately a breaking with charity, a failure to love. Because of that, what matters most is that we learn to love again after we've failed.

It is always important to say "I'm sorry" when we've hurt someone. And not just in words, but through a hug, a kind gesture, or a simple act of encouragement. In the words of the Carmelite mystic St. John of the Cross in his *Sayings of Light and Love*: "In the evening of life, we will be judged on love alone." Learning to forgive and reconcile is one of the most important lessons in our family. It is a small but powerful way to keep love at the center of our home.

## Mercy in the Life of Christ

The Gospels overflow with mercy:

- Jesus forgave Peter after his denial (John 21:15–17).
- He revealed the Father's mercy through the parable of the prodigal son (Luke 15).
- He fed the hungry out of compassion (Matthew 15:32).

And from the Cross, his greatest act of mercy: "Father, forgive them, for they know not what they do" (Luke 23:34).

These are not just stories of the past. They are reminders that Christ looks at us with the same tenderness today. His mercy is new every morning.

## Mercy in Family Life

When we pray, "Lord, have mercy. Christ, have mercy," we are not only asking for ourselves. We are also asking that mercy fill our homes. Families need mercy daily: when tempers flare, when words wound, when misunderstandings arise.

Mercy means being willing to forgive quickly, to apologize sincerely, and to see one another through God's eyes. Just as the Holy Family lived in patience and love, our families, too, are called to be little Nazareths, places where mercy is practiced in the ordinary moments of life.

**Practical ways families can live mercy:**

- **Begin each day with a simple prayer:** "Jesus, have mercy on us and help us to forgive one another today."
- **Practice reconciliation at home:** End the day with apologies and blessings before bed.
- **Mercy Jar:** Place slips of paper in a jar where family members can write encouraging words or "thank yous" for acts of love and mercy they've noticed. Read them together once a week. This balances asking forgiveness with celebrating love.

## Closing Prayer

Lord Jesus, You are Mercy itself.
Teach us to see our sins clearly, but to see your mercy even more. Fill our homes with forgiveness and peace.
Help us to treat each other with patience, to forgive quickly, and to love deeply.
May our families become places where your mercy is always alive.
Amen.

## Reflection Questions

- Where have I experienced God's mercy most deeply in my life?

## Day 1: Mercy at the Heart of the Gospel

- How can I show mercy to a family member today in a small, concrete way?
- What keeps me from forgiving quickly, and how can I invite Christ into that struggle?

# DAY 2

# Trusting His Providence

*Christ, hear us. Christ, graciously hear us.*

## Opening Scripture

"And this is the confidence which we have in him, that if we ask anything according to his will he hears us." *(1 John 5:14)*

## Christ Who Listens

Every line of the Litany is both prayer and proclamation. When we say, "Christ, hear us. Christ, graciously hear us," we are not crying out into the void. We are speaking to the living Lord who listens with a heart of mercy.

From his time on earth until now, Jesus has never turned away from those who cry out to him. The Gospels are full of moments when people sought his help: the blind calling out, the sick reaching to touch his cloak, parents begging for their children's healing. He stopped, He listened, He answered.

There was a season when my family and I (five of us living in a small apartment) deeply longed for a home of our own. For me, it was more than just the dream of a house; I had never known homeownership growing up and longed to give my children stability.

After months of searching, we finally found what felt like our dream home and placed a strong offer. At first, we were told it would be ours. Then another buyer outbid us with an amount we couldn't match. My heart sank, and it felt as though our prayers had been in vain.

In my disappointment, I turned again to prayer. I began a novena to St. Joseph that providentially ended on his feast day, March 19. Each day, my husband and I prayed, asking Jesus, through Joseph's intercession, to grant us this house if it was God's will. It seemed impossible, but we trusted.

On the ninth day, March 19, the house unexpectedly came back on the market. The other buyer had backed out. By God's grace, and with St. Joseph's intercession, the house became ours. Even more beautifully, we closed on the Feast of St. Gianna Molla, another saint dear to our family.

Through this experience, I learned again that Christ truly does hear us, even when his answer comes through waiting, anticipation, or in ways we do not expect. His providence always works things out at the right time.

## Christ's Intercession

On the Cross, Jesus' prayer reached its deepest expression: "Father, forgive them, for they know not what they do" (Luke 23:34). His intercession was not only for those present at Calvary but for all people, for all time.

After his Resurrection and Ascension, Scripture tells us that he continues this intercession: "Christ Jesus ... is at the right hand of God, who indeed intercedes for us" (Romans 8:34). Even now, every prayer we offer reaches his merciful heart.

## Trusting His Answer

When we pray, "Christ, graciously hear us," we affirm that he not only hears but responds with love. Sometimes his answer comes quickly; sometimes it comes slowly; sometimes it comes in ways we did not expect. But always, his response flows from divine wisdom and mercy.

As families, this trust is often tested through financial strain, illness, conflict, or uncertainty. Yet each of these moments can become opportunities to say, "Christ, hear us," and then rest in the assurance that he is guiding us according to the Father's loving plan.

## Living This Prayer as Families

- **Begin the Day Together:** Start mornings with the invocation, "Christ, hear us. Christ, graciously hear us," offering to him your family's hopes and needs.

- **Keep a Prayer Journal:** Write down intentions and revisit them each month. Note how God has answered, not always as expected, but always with love.
- **In Times of Delay:** When prayers seem unanswered, follow Mary's example of pondering in her heart (Luke 2:19). Ask, "What is Christ teaching us in this waiting?"
- **Unite Prayers to the Cross:** Invite family members to silently place their worries at the foot of the Cross, remembering his words: "By His wounds we are healed" (Isaiah 53:5).

## Closing Prayer

Lord, you are goodness itself.
You who listened to the cries of the poor and
    the pleas of the suffering, hear us now with
    your merciful Heart.
Teach us to trust your answers, even when they
    differ from our desires.
Help our families rest in your providence,
    knowing that you never abandon those
    who call upon you.
Christ, hear us. Christ, graciously hear us.
Amen.

## Reflection Questions

- When have I felt most confident that Christ heard my prayer?

## Day 2: Trusting His Providence

- How do I usually respond when my prayers are not answered as I hoped?
- What prayer can my family bring to Christ together this week, trusting His mercy?

DAY 3

# The Father's Merciful Heart

*God, the Father of Heaven, have mercy on us.*

## Opening Scripture

"As a father pities his children, so the Lord pities those who fear him." *(Psalm 103:13)*

## The Tender Heart of the Father

When we call upon "God, the Father of Heaven," we are turning to the source of all creation, who is not distant but tender, merciful, and close. From the beginning, God has shown his people that his fatherhood is marked not by severity but by steadfast love. He is the Father who provides manna in the desert, who carries his children through exile, who never forgets his promises.

Jesus revealed this even more deeply when he taught us to say, "Our Father." The God who created the stars invites us to call him Abba, a word of intimacy, trust, and closeness.

## The Prodigal Son

Of all Jesus' parables, none illustrates the Father's mercy more beautifully than the story of the Prodigal Son (Luke 15:11–32). The father in the story does not wait for explanations. He runs to meet his wayward child, embracing him before a single apology is spoken.

This parable shows us that God is not a Father who holds grudges but one who opens his arms to welcome us home. His mercy is extravagant, restoring us with dignity, clothing us in love, and preparing a feast for our return.

For our family, we encounter this mercy most profoundly in the sacrament of confession. We are all prodigal children in need of forgiveness, and in the confessional, God the Father waits for us with open arms. When our children were first old enough for confession, they felt embarrassed to admit their sins aloud. I told them, "This is where you meet Jesus. It is Jesus, through the priest, who forgives you and shows you the Father's face."

Over the years, as we have gone consistently as a family, I have witnessed a change. What once felt intimidating has become a place of freedom. Now my children are the ones to say, "Can we go to confession this week?" There is something mystical that happens in the sacrament. Christ Himself not only wipes away our sins but gives us grace to resist them in the future. In this way, the confessional becomes our own encounter with the merciful Father. Just like the son in the parable, we come with nothing but our weakness, and yet we leave restored, embraced, and strengthened by the love of God.

## Fatherly Mercy in Our Homes

The Father's mercy is not only something we receive; it is something we are called to reflect. Parents mirror God's compassion when they discipline with patience, forgive quickly, and provide generously. Children reflect his mercy when they respect, listen, and offer trust.

**Practical ways to reflect the Father's mercy as a family:**

- **Daily Our Father:** Pray slowly as a family, pausing at "forgive us as we forgive."
- **Practice Quick Forgiveness:** Don't let anger linger overnight. Make reconciliation a habit before bedtime.
- **Signs of Reassurance:** Parents can echo God's mercy with simple gestures. Offer an embrace after correction, a kind word after conflict, or reassurance of love.

In these small ways, the mercy of God the Father becomes alive within the walls of our homes.

## Closing Prayer

Heavenly Father,
You are mercy itself.
Teach us to trust you as children trust their parents.
Forgive us when we stray, and help us reflect your compassion in our families.
Make our homes places of welcome and reconciliation,
where love is stronger than anger, and forgiveness flows freely.
Amen.

## Reflection Questions

- How do I imagine God the Father: distant or close, stern or merciful?
- What does the parable of the Prodigal Son teach me about how God looks at me?
- How can my family imitate the Father's mercy toward one another this week?

DAY 4

## Mercy Made Present

*God the Son, Redeemer of the world, have mercy on us.*

### Opening Scripture

"For God so loved the world that he gave his only Son, that whoever believes in him should not perish but have eternal life." *(John 3:16)*

### The Redeemer's Love

When we pray, "God the Son, Redeemer of the world, have mercy on us," we proclaim the heart of the Christian faith: Jesus Christ gave His life to save us. He is not only the Savior of history but the living Redeemer who enters our daily struggles, offering forgiveness, healing, and peace.

From Bethlehem to Calvary, Jesus revealed mercy in action. He healed the sick, welcomed the sinner, lifted up the poor, and forgave His enemies. On the cross, His love reached its fullest expression as He bore our sins and washed them away. Through His Resurrection, He broke the chains of death so that every family could share in the hope of new life.

## Mercy Poured Out

The mercy of Christ is not confined to the past; it is alive today. We encounter His redeeming love most powerfully in the sacraments:

- **The Eucharist:** At every Mass, Jesus gives Himself to us in His Body and Blood. Families who receive Him together are strengthened in unity, patience, and love.
- **Reconciliation (Confession):** In this sacrament, Jesus forgives our sins and restores our hearts. Families who practice confession regularly learn humility, honesty, and the joy of mercy received.

Each time we approach these sacraments, Christ the Redeemer meets us personally, reminding us that His mercy is always available.

For our family, the Eucharist is at the very heart of our life of faith. We attend Sunday Mass faithfully and, whenever possible, weekday Mass as well. We try to teach our children that the Mass is not something we simply "watch." It is something we enter into with our whole hearts. To help them pray more deeply, we encourage them to unite their trials and difficulties to the Cross of Christ.

In particular, I often tell them that during the moment of transubstantiation (when the bread becomes the body of Christ, and the wine becomes his blood), we are spiritually standing at the foot of Calvary. When the priest raises the Host and then the chalice, we invite our children to silently place their intentions on the altar: their struggles, hopes, and prayers, whether big or small. Spiritually, we unite our prayers to Jesus' perfect offering on the cross. This is one of the most powerful intercessions we have as Catholics, because it unites our prayers to Christ's perfect sacrifice.

I often remind our children of the words of Jesus to St. Faustina Kowalska in her *Diary: Divine Mercy in My Soul*: "One drop alone of My Blood would have been enough for the salvation of the world" (paraphrased from Diary, 72). Faustina, the Polish nun to whom Jesus entrusted the Divine Mercy devotion, often wrote about the limitless power of his mercy poured out through his passion and the sacraments. This devotion shows that the smallest act of trust in him can unleash immense grace. If one drop of his precious blood is enough to redeem the world, then we can trust that every prayer, burden, and intention we place into the chalice at Mass is embraced by God's mercy. The Eucharist is thus not only Christ's gift of himself to us but also his invitation to entrust everything into the infinite wellspring of his redeeming love.

Over time, I've seen this practice change the way our children approach Mass. They are learning that their prayers matter, that nothing is too small to bring to Jesus, and that every Mass is an opportunity to hand everything over to the Redeemer of the world. In this way, the Eucharist becomes not only a moment of communion but a living experience of Christ's mercy, binding our family more closely to him and to one another.

## Living Christ's Redemption at Home

To call Jesus our Redeemer is to trust that his love can transform family life. He redeems our impatience with his patience, our anger with his peace, our hurts with his healing.

**Practical ways families can live Christ's redeeming mercy:**

- Pray the Divine Mercy Chaplet together, especially during times of stress or conflict.
- Practice small sacrifices in daily life: helping with chores without complaint, listening patiently, or offering kind words in place of criticism.
- Celebrate reconciliation at home: Encourage apologies and forgiveness quickly, reflecting Jesus' desire to restore us to peace.
- Keep Christ at the center: Place a crucifix in a visible place in the home as a reminder of his redeeming love.

## Closing Prayer

> Lord Jesus, Redeemer of the world,
> You gave your life so that we might live.
> Enter our homes with your mercy,
> Heal our wounds, and restore our peace.
> Teach us to forgive as you forgive, and to love
>     as you love.
> May our families be renewed each day by your
>     saving grace.
> Amen.

## Reflection Questions

- How do I experience Christ as my Redeemer in daily life?
- What areas of my family life most need his healing mercy?
- How can I bring the mercy of Jesus to others this week through words, actions, or forgiveness?

# DAY 5

# The Spirit's Gentle Presence

*God the Holy Spirit, have mercy on us.*

## Opening Scripture

"But the Counselor, the Holy Spirit, whom the Father will send in my name, he will teach you all things, and bring to your remembrance all that I have said to you." *(John 14:26)*

## The Bond of Love

When we pray, "God the Holy Spirit, have mercy on us," we are asking for the presence of the one who guides, comforts, and sanctifies. The Spirit is not distant or abstract. He is the breath of God, alive and active in our lives, ready to strengthen families with peace, courage, and love.

From Pentecost onward, the Spirit has been the life of the Church. He gave the apostles boldness, filled them with joy, and united them in mission. Today, he longs to do the same for us: to empower our families to live in harmony and to shine as witnesses of God's mercy.

This same Spirit, who animates the Church from Pentecost onward, was understood by St. Bonaventure as the *nexus amoris*. This Latin phrase means the living bond of love between the Father and the Son, the Person in whom their eternal gift of self is perfectly expressed (*Breviloquium*, I.10.2). In this sense, the Holy Spirit is Love in person. The family mirrors this mystery in a particular way: the love of husband and wife, poured out in fidelity, becomes fruitful and life-giving, reflecting the Trinitarian communion. Just as the Spirit is the unifying Love who binds the Father and Son, in the family, love becomes the bond that holds persons together and generates new life. Thus, the family is rightly called both the "domestic church" (CCC, 2204) and the "original cell of social life" (CCC, 2207), where the love of God is made visible and shared in daily life.

## Mercy Through the Spirit

The Holy Spirit's mercy is revealed in the quiet ways he works in our hearts:

- He softens pride and prompts us to forgive.
- He gives courage to say, "I'm sorry."

- He brings comfort when we feel discouraged.
- He inspires acts of kindness that heal family wounds.

The Spirit also fills us with His gifts (wisdom, understanding, counsel, fortitude, knowledge, piety, and fear of the Lord) and cultivates fruits in us: love, joy, peace, patience, kindness, goodness, faithfulness, gentleness, and self-control (Galatians 5:22–23). These are not abstract virtues; they are signs that mercy is alive in our homes.

I remember one evening when two of my children were not getting along, and neither wanted to admit fault. The room was filled with silence after the argument, each one stubbornly holding their ground. After a few minutes, one of them quietly came over to me and said, "Mom, I think the Holy Spirit is telling me to say I'm sorry." With that, they went to their sibling, spoke the words, and within minutes, the two of them were hugging and laughing again as if nothing had happened.

In our family, we often talk about how saying "I'm sorry" first is really an act of humility, one of the most important virtues for family life and for getting along with others. I tell my children that even if they weren't the ones who started the conflict, it is always important to acknowledge their own faults without judging the other person. That first step of humility opens the door for peace and reconciliation.

That evening showed me again how the Holy Spirit works in whispers, softening hearts and giving the courage to take the first step toward forgiveness. What could have remained an evening of stubbornness and hurt feelings became, instead, a small victory of grace.

**Practical ways families can welcome the Spirit's mercy:**

- Pray, "Come, Holy Spirit" daily, before meals, bedtime, or family decisions.
- Use the fruits of the Spirit as a family "examination of conscience," reflecting together on how love, patience, or kindness were practiced that week.
- Pause in conflict: In tense moments, stop to pray, "Holy Spirit, bring us peace." Even a brief prayer can calm hearts and open paths to forgiveness.
- Serve together: Ask, "Holy Spirit, where can we show mercy today?" Then visit a neighbor, call someone who is lonely, or volunteer as a family.

These simple practices make room for the Spirit to transform ordinary moments into holy ones.

## Closing Prayer

Holy Spirit,
You are the Comforter and Guide.
Fill our hearts with your peace, soften our
    words with gentleness,
and make our home a place of mercy.
Teach us to listen for your promptings, to
    forgive quickly, and to serve joyfully.
Come, Holy Spirit, dwell in us always.
Amen.

# Day 5: The Spirit's Gentle Presence

## Reflection Questions

- Where do I see the fruits of the Spirit already at work in my family?
- How can I invite the Spirit more intentionally into my daily choices?
- What is one concrete way our family can show mercy this week with the Spirit's help?

DAY 6

# The Mystery of Love

*Holy Trinity, one God, have mercy on us.*

## Opening Scripture

"Go therefore and make disciples of all nations, baptizing them in the name of the Father and of the Son and of the Holy Spirit." *(Matthew 28:19)*

## The Trinity of Mercy

When we pray, "Holy Trinity, one God, have mercy on us," we speak to the deepest mystery of our faith. God is one, yet three Persons (Father, Son, and Holy Spirit) perfectly united in love. This truth is not only for theologians; it is the foundation of

Christian life. The Trinity is a living communion of love, and we are invited to reflect that love in our families.

God the Father shows mercy in his providence. God the Son redeems us through his sacrifice. God the Holy Spirit renews us with his gifts. Together, they reveal that mercy is not something God does occasionally; it is who he is.

## A Family Shaped by the Trinity

The life of the Trinity can be mirrored in the home. Just as Father, Son, and Spirit are united in love, families are called to live in harmony, even in the midst of differences. When parents forgive quickly, when children respect and listen, when siblings encourage instead of criticize, the family becomes a small reflection of the Trinity's unity.

I remember one Saturday when our family decided to tackle a big project at home. My husband and I worked together on outdoor tasks, while the kids took on organizing toys, sporting equipment, and even putting art supplies back in order inside. Eventually, we all came together to tackle the kitchen, my least favorite job. At first, there were groans, complaints, and even some arguments about who had the harder task. But slowly, something began to change. Each person settled into their work, and little by little, the house began to take shape.

By the end of the day, the toys were in bins, the books were stacked neatly on shelves, the art supplies were sorted, the kitchen was cleaner, and the outside looked refreshed. Standing back, I realized that what felt like chaos at first had come together into something beautiful. It reminded me of a stained-glass window.

Up close, the pieces look scattered and broken, but when fit together and illuminated, they reveal a pattern of light and beauty.

St. Paul teaches, "As a body is one though it has many members, and all the members of the body, though many, are one body" (1 Corinthians 12:12). That day, our family project became more than chores; it was a glimpse of what happens when each person contributes their gifts for the good of the whole. In its own imperfect way, it mirrored the mystery of the Trinity: Father, Son, and Holy Spirit, each distinct, yet perfectly united in love.

**Practical ways families can live the mercy of the Trinity:**

- **Pray reflecting on the Trinity:** Begin and end each day with the Sign of the Cross, remembering that you belong to Father, Son, and Spirit.
- **Create unity through listening:** Hold family conversations where each member is heard and valued, echoing the Trinity's perfect communion.
- **Forgive and reconcile:** Imitate God's unity by working through conflicts quickly. Unity grows when mercy is practiced.
- **Celebrate together:** Share meals, prayers, and joys as reminders that love multiplies when it is lived communally.

## Closing Prayer

> Holy Trinity (Father, Son, and Holy Spirit),
> You are perfect unity and perfect love.
> Pour out your mercy upon our family.
> Teach us to forgive as you forgive, to love as you love,
> and to live in harmony with one another.
> Make our home a reflection of your eternal communion,
> so that all who enter may glimpse the mercy of God.
> Amen.

## Reflection Questions

- How does the love between the Father, Son, and Holy Spirit inspire the way I treat my family?
- In what moments has my family reflected the unity and harmony of the Trinity?
- How can I bring mercy into situations of conflict so that unity is restored?

## DAY 7

# The Communion of Prayer

*Jesus, Mary, and Joseph, pray for us.*

## Opening Scripture

"The prayer of a righteous man has great power in its effects." *(James 5:16)*

## Interceding with Jesus, Mary, and Joseph

Prayer is never a solitary act. When we whisper a need in the quiet of our hearts, that prayer rises with that of countless others before God's throne. Every prayer echoes the prayer of Christ himself, who intercedes before the Father for all creation.

According to the Catechism of the Catholic Church, "intercession is a prayer of petition which leads us to pray as Jesus did" (CCC 2634). Prayer itself is "the raising of one's mind and heart to God" (CCC 2559). It is a living relationship with the Lord that expresses humility, trust, and love. When we intercede, we ask God to hear us. We also participate in the love of Christ, who "lives always to make intercession" for us (Hebrews 7:25).

From the beginning, Scripture shows how God delights when His people pray for one another. Moses pleaded for Israel's forgiveness after they turned from the covenant, and the Lord relented (Exodus 32:11–14). Samuel promised never to cease praying for his people, knowing that intercession was an act of love and fidelity (1 Samuel 12:23). Job prayed for his friends, and the Lord restored them (Job 42:10). In the Acts of the Apostles, the early Church prayed earnestly for Peter while he was in prison, and God sent an angel to release him (Acts 12:5).

When we pray, "Jesus, Mary, and Joseph, pray for us," we stand within this same sacred tradition. We join our petitions to the communion of saints, trusting that those who are perfectly united with God in heaven continue to intercede for us in love. God delights in such prayer because it mirrors his mercy and draws us deeper into communion with one another.

## The Communion of Saints

The Church teaches that we are united with all who belong to Christ: those on earth, in purgatory, and in heaven (CCC 946–959). Just as we ask friends and loved ones to pray for us, we can also ask the saints. Their intercession participates in Christ's one mediation (1 Timothy 2:5) and never replaces it; rather, their prayers flow from his saving work and draw us deeper into his love.

The Holy Family holds a special place in this communion. Joseph and Mary were so closely bound to Jesus that their prayers now echo His own mercy for us. Because of their nearness to Him, the Church has always turned to them with confidence: Mary as our mother, Joseph as our protector, and Jesus as our Savior and Lord.

This reality reminds us that the Church is never limited to what we see on Sunday in our parish. We are surrounded by "a great cloud of witnesses" (Hebrews 12:1) who encourage us, strengthen us, and intercede for us as we run the race of faith. The saints in heaven cheer us on, those in purgatory are purified in God's mercy, and we on earth lift one another up through prayer.

The Holy Family stands at the heart of this mystery. When we invoke them, we are reminded that heaven and earth are not far apart but joined in Christ. Our homes become little echoes of this communion when we pray for one another and entrust our needs to the intercession of the saints.

## A Family Story of Intercession

The communion of saints reminds us that no one prays or suffers alone. Heaven, purgatory, and earth are mysteriously bound together in Christ's love. Our family once learned this truth during a difficult Christmas season years ago. My husband was finishing graduate school, and I was home with three little ones: a baby, a preschooler, and a kindergartener. We were struggling to keep up with the bills, let alone think about gifts under the tree.

Each night we began to pray as a family for others who might be facing housing or food insecurity. A wise friend had once told me that one secret to having your own prayers answered is to pray for others going through the same thing. Then, just a few weeks before Christmas, an unexpected envelope arrived in the mail with a generous gift from someone in our parish who had quietly heard of our situation. In that moment, I felt as though God himself had reached into our little Nazareth to remind us that He sees, He provides, and He answers, just in time. In praying for others, God had answered ours. Heaven responded through a heart made generous by his grace.

That moment reminded me of the Holy Family in Bethlehem. In the city of David, Mary and Joseph held the Infant Jesus in such humble circumstances, trusting entirely in God's providence. Christ, who once lay in the manger as an innocent newborn, is the very Word through whom all things were made (John 1:3). The same Lord who fashioned the heavens and the earth continues to provide for His children, often in ways that surprise us.

## Trusting in Mary and Joseph's Care

Mary's intercession is tender and attentive. At Cana, she saw a need before anyone else and brought it to Jesus. She does the same for us today, noticing what we lack and whispering to her

Son on our behalf. Her role is never to replace Him but to lead us closer to Him.

As Mary leads us by her words, Joseph guides us by his silence. Joseph, though silent in Scripture, speaks through his actions. He obeyed God's messages in dreams, protected Mary and Jesus, and provided for them faithfully. The Church has long recognized his powerful patronage, calling him the Patron of the Universal Church. His intercession is especially strong for fathers, workers, and families who struggle quietly with daily burdens.

## Living Intercession at Home

The Holy Family's example invites us to practice intercession in our own families. Just as they pray for us, we are called to pray for each other. Parents can pray for children, children for parents, and siblings for one another. Prayer is not only words but acts of love that lift up those around us.

**Ways to bring this into family life:**

- End the day with each family member offering one prayer intention aloud.
- Create a family "intercession list" and place it near a home prayer corner.
- Encourage children to pray for teachers or friends in need, forming habits of compassion early.

When we intercede for one another, we participate in God's mercy and reflect the care of Jesus, Mary, and Joseph. In this way, our homes become small sanctuaries of intercession, where the love of the Holy Family takes root. In the stillness of prayer, heaven bends toward every home that calls upon the names of Jesus, Mary, and Joseph.

## Closing Prayer

> Jesus, Mary, and Joseph, pray for our families.
> Bring our needs before the Father's throne.
> Teach us to intercede with love for one another,
> to notice the needs around us, and to carry
> > them to God with trust.
> Make our homes places of prayerful mercy,
> > where no one is forgotten.
> Amen.

## Reflection Questions

- How has someone's prayer or intercession made a difference in my life?
- Do I regularly pray for my family members' needs? How could I begin or grow in this?
- How can my family become more like the Holy Family in noticing and responding to the needs of others?

WEEK 2

# The Journey of Faith

## DAY 8

# Honoring the Holy Family

*Jesus, Mary, and Joseph, most worthy
of our veneration, pray for us.*

## Opening Scripture

"Honor your father and your mother, that your days may be long in the land which the Lord your God gives you." *(Exodus 20:12)*

## What Does Veneration Mean?

True honor begins in the heart. The Fourth Commandment reminds us that reverence for those God has placed in our lives opens our hearts to reverence for Him.

When we pray, "Jesus, Mary, and Joseph, most worthy of our veneration," we are honoring the way God's grace worked in their lives. In Catholic tradition, veneration means showing deep respect for those who reflect God's holiness. We worship God alone, but we honor Mary, Joseph, and the saints because their lives lead us closer to Him.

The Church distinguishes between *latria* (the worship owed to God alone) and *dulia* (the veneration offered to the saints). Mary receives a unique honor called *hyperdulia*, for her singular cooperation with God's grace in bringing forth the Savior. We adore God alone, and we venerate Mary and the saints, honoring God's work in them.

Elizabeth's greeting to Mary, "Blessed are you among women" (Luke 1:42), is one of the first examples of veneration in Scripture. Respecting those who live faithfully is not about elevating them above God, but about recognizing how God shines through them.

## A Family Worthy of Honor

Each member of the Holy Family reveals something of God's own heart:

- **Jesus:** As true God and true Man, Jesus is adored with worship due only to God. He humbled himself, became one of us, and gave His life in obedience to the Father's will (Philippians 2:8).
- **Mary:** She is honored above all creatures for her yes to God. From the Annunciation to the Cross, she trust-

ed, pondered, and prayed. Her faith and contemplation guide us in following Christ.
- **Joseph:** Silent in Scripture yet powerful in action, Joseph guarded Mary and Jesus with steadfast faith. His humble obedience and diligent work sanctify ordinary family life.

Each member of the Holy Family mirrors a virtue we can imitate: Jesus in his charity, Mary in her faith, and Joseph in his trust.

## Growing Closer Through Veneration

Venerating the Holy Family is not only about images or feast days; it is about imitating their virtues in the ordinary pace of life.

**Ways to bring this into family life:**

- Pray the Rosary together, reflecting on Christ's life through Mary's eyes.
- Celebrate feast days of Mary or Joseph with a simple family meal.
- Offer your daily work to God as Joseph did, transforming ordinary tasks into prayer.
- Practice small acts of honor at home: listening with attention, thanking one another, speaking with respect.

When we show honor to one another in love, we learn the pattern of veneration itself, seeing Christ present in those God has entrusted to us.

## A Family Story of Veneration

Our family has always loved Christmas. We are usually one of the last families in the neighborhood to take down the outdoor lights, and while we pack away the tree, wreaths, and decorations, one thing always stays out just a little longer: the Nativity scene. Over the years it has become the centerpiece of our Christmas celebrations, and we've tried to teach our children that the crèche is not just another decoration, but a sacred reminder of the Holy Family's love.

The highlight is always placing the baby Jesus in the manger on Christmas morning. He is tiny, barely the size of a child's pinkie finger, yet somehow he becomes the heart of the whole season. One year, however, we misplaced the baby Jesus. We searched everywhere, but he was nowhere to be found. Christmas morning felt strangely incomplete without him in the crèche, and months later, we finally found him hidden in a drawer. I felt an almost overwhelming relief in placing him back in the manger. I couldn't bear to pack the Nativity away until I found him.

That small absence became a quiet parable. When we lose sight of Jesus, even our celebrations feel hollow. True veneration always begins with finding him again at the center.

That moment reminded me how Mary and Joseph teach us what it means to reverence Christ, even in his littleness. Just as they cared for our Lord in Bethlehem with love and tenderness, we too are called to keep Jesus at the center of our homes, honoring him with the same devotion.

## Closing Prayer

> Jesus, Mary, and Joseph,
> most worthy of our veneration,
> teach us to honor you by honoring one
>     another.
> Help us imitate the obedience, trust, and love
>     you shared within your home at Nazareth.
> Through your intercession,
> may our homes reflect holiness
> and draw us closer to the Father's mercy.
> Amen.

## Reflection Questions

- How do I understand the difference between veneration and worship?
- Which member of the Holy Family do I feel closest to in prayer right now, and why?
- How can my family show greater honor and respect to one another in daily life?

# DAY 9

# God's Eternal Plan

*Jesus, Mary, and Joseph, chosen as the Holy Family from all time, pray for us.*

## Opening Scripture

"He chose us in him before the foundation of the world, to be holy and blameless before him in love." *(Ephesians 1:4)*

## Set Apart from the Beginning

When we call upon "the Holy Family from all time," we are reminded that Jesus, Mary, and Joseph were not brought together by chance. From all eternity, in His providence, God planned their role in salvation history. Though they lived in a specific time and culture, their holiness transcends centuries. Their witness is a model for every family in every age.

God prepared this family so that the Word could take flesh in the midst of ordinary life. Their unity, love, and trust reveal that God's plan has always been to bring holiness into the heart of the home. And if God prepared them from all eternity, He also prepares us (our families, our marriages, and our children) to walk in His grace, even when we cannot yet see the road ahead.

This verse reminds us that holiness is not accidental. God's plan of love, from before the world began, included the family through whom His Son would enter the world.

## What Makes a Family Holy

A holy family is not one without struggles, but one that places God at the center. Holiness doesn't erase hardship; it transforms it.

Jesus reminds us: "You shall love the Lord your God with all your heart, and with all your soul, and with all your mind. This is the great and first commandment. And a second is like it: You shall love your neighbor as yourself." (Matthew 22:37–39)

Mary and Joseph faced unexpected journeys, hard decisions, and moments of sorrow:

- Fleeing to Egypt in the middle of the night to protect the infant Jesus.
- Hearing Simeon's prophecy that a sword would pierce Mary's heart.
- Searching anxiously for Him for three days in Jerusalem.

Yet their trust in God transformed these trials into opportunities of grace.

Holiness is not lived in grand gestures but in daily faithfulness. It shows up in the ordinary routines of family life: going to work because the family depends on God working through you to provide; driving children to practices or lessons, waiting in the parking lot, and bringing them safely home, just as Mary and Joseph made countless unseen journeys with Jesus. Holiness is choosing to do what delights your child, even when you would never choose it yourself, like watching the same cartoon again, sitting through another long sports meet, or listening attentively to their latest fascination with dinosaurs, trains, or unicorns. These hidden sacrifices echo Nazareth, where Jesus grew "in wisdom and in stature, and in favor with God and man" (Luke 2:52).

## A Family Story of Holiness

We are a homeschooling family, but for one school year a few years ago, we discerned that the best choice for our children was placing them in a private school. At the time they were struggling with homeschooling (paying attention, following through, and practicing obedience), so we decided to show them another way of learning. We found a school that seemed perfect, checking all the boxes, and the kids were thrilled to go.

What I hadn't realized until after we signed the contracts and paid the tuition was just how demanding the commute would be. Though the school was less than an hour away "as the crow flies," the traffic in our area turned it into nearly a four-hour round trip every single day. I absolutely dreaded that drive, yet I did it out of love for my children. Many times, as I gripped the steering wheel and sipped my lukewarm coffee, I thought of St. Joseph leading Mary (pregnant with Jesus) over long and difficult miles.

Their quiet endurance sanctified the road, and in a small way, I learned that holiness can be hidden in long commutes, tired mornings, and daily sacrifices no one else sees. In those weary hours, I began to understand that holiness is often hidden on the long road: quiet, faithful, and unseen.

## Families of Every Shape

Every family (whether large or small, traditional or blended, joyful or grieving) can mirror Nazareth when love, patience, and mercy guide their relationships. On the Cross, Jesus gave Mary to John, forming a family not bound by blood but by faith and love. So too, every family that welcomes Christ into its heart shares in His holiness. In that moment, Jesus revealed that family is not only about shared ancestry but about shared fidelity to God.

Even Jesus Himself said in Scripture: "Who is my mother, and who are my brethren? For whoever does the will of my Father in heaven is my brother, and sister, and mother." (Matthew 12:48, 50)

The bonds of love, forgiveness, and sacrifice can make any home (even one that feels broken or imperfect) a true dwelling place of God's presence.

**Practical ways families can grow in holiness:**

- **Prayer:** Even five quiet minutes of prayer before breakfast can reset the whole day.
- **Forgiveness:** Don't let small conflicts harden hearts. A simple Hail Mary together can soften anger.
- **Service:** The hidden sacrifices (whether a long commute or a chore done in silence) become holy when offered in love.
- **Sacraments:** Sunday Mass and regular Confession renew our families with grace and strength for the journey.

Holiness is not perfection, but faithfulness. The Holy Family shows us that God's presence can sanctify the most ordinary moments.

## Closing Prayer

Lord God,
You who destined Jesus, Mary, and Joseph to
    be the Holy Family from all eternity,
teach our families to reflect their unity, love,
    and trust in Your plan.
Help us to welcome Your grace in daily life, to
    forgive freely,
to serve generously,
and to grow in holiness together.
Make our homes another Nazareth, where
    Christ is welcomed with joy.
Amen.

## Reflection Questions

- What does it mean that God prepared the Holy Family from all time?
- Where in my family's life is God already present, and where do I need to invite Him more intentionally?
- What is one small way we can grow in holiness together this week?

## DAY 10

# Distinct Roles, One Unity

*Jesus, Mary, and Joseph, son, mother, and head of the Holy Family, pray for us.*

## Opening Scripture

"Children, obey your parents in the Lord, for this is right. 'Honor your father and mother,' this is the first commandment with a promise." *(Ephesians 6:1–2)*

## United in Purpose

When we pray this line of the Litany, we recall the unique yet complementary roles of Jesus, Mary, and Joseph. Jesus is the obedient Son, Mary the devoted Mother, and Joseph the faithful head of the Holy Family. Together, their lives show us how God sanctifies family life and reveals His love through ordinary roles lived faithfully.

- **Jesus as Son:** Though He is the eternal Son of God, Jesus also freely submitted to Mary and Joseph in Nazareth: "And he went down with them and came to Nazareth, and was obedient to them" (Luke 2:51). In this humility, He teaches children the dignity of obedience and the holiness of family life.
- **Mary as Mother:** Mary nurtured Jesus in faith, prayer, and daily care. Her motherhood was both physical and spiritual, nurturing the faith of her household and modeling total receptivity to God. Her Magnificat reveals her heart of gratitude and trust, and her maternal guidance always pointed toward her Son. At the wedding feast of Cana, she told the servants, "Do whatever he tells you" (John 2:5). In this simple command, Mary models what every Christian parent longs to do: lead their children and household to listen to Christ above all else.
- **Joseph as Head:** Joseph protected and provided for his family with humility and strength. Scripture says, "For the husband is the head of the wife as Christ is the head of the church, his body" (Ephesians 5:23). This headship does not mean domination or control; rather, it means a call to sacrificial love. Just as Christ laid down His life for the Church, Joseph laid down his life daily for Mary and Jesus. His leadership shone through service, integrity, and quiet faithfulness.

Each role (Son, Mother, and Head) reveals a different facet of holiness, yet together they form one united household of love.

## Lessons for Families Today

The Holy Family reminds us that holiness is not perfection but faithfulness. Their unity came from prayer, trust, and mutual respect. Jesus Himself, though the eternal Son of God, accepted obedience to His earthly parents. In doing so, He dignified family authority and showed that love often means surrendering our own will for the good of another.

Through His obedience, Jesus dignified every act of family love and transformed duty into devotion. Scripture underscores this truth: "Honor your father and your mother, that your days may be prolonged" (Deuteronomy 5:16), and again, "Children, obey your parents in everything, for this pleases the Lord" (Colossians 3:20). These words remind us that obedience is not merely about rules; it is about love, and it carries the promise of blessing.

In our own homes, obedience is often tested in daily moments that stretch our patience. In my family, I am the cook. One of the hardest things is when I spend so much time calling and calling my children to the table, only to be met with silence. I know they must hear me, but they are wrapped up in something else. What fills me with gratitude is when I call, and they come immediately. That simple act of obedience is more than good manners; it is an act of love. It mirrors the respect Jesus gave to Mary and Joseph, and it also reminds me, as a parent, to show patience, to give clear guidance, and to model respect in return.

Like Mary, parents are called to nurture through love, not harshness. Like Joseph, fathers and guardians are called to provide and protect with quiet strength. And like Jesus, children are called to respond with honor and obedience, even when it costs them something. When these roles are lived faithfully, the home becomes a reflection of Nazareth.

## A Word on Headship

When we speak of the father as the "head" of the family, we understand it in the Christian framework, not as power or control, but as a call to sacrificial love. As St. Paul teaches, "For the husband is the head of the wife as Christ is the head of the church" (Ephesians 5:23). Headship, then, is modeled after Christ, who gave His life for His Bride, the Church. A father leads not by demanding service, but by serving first.

Yet many families today do not have a father present. Some are led by single mothers, grandparents, or other guardians. God's grace remains sufficient for every home. Authority in the family, rightly understood, is entrusted to the parent or guardian present, and children honor them by their obedience. In these situations, mothers too carry the role of guiding, protecting, and nurturing. Obedience to parents, then, is not blind submission, but a response of love and respect to those God has placed in authority. Every act of love that protects, provides, or forgives participates in the fatherhood of God. Holiness is found not in a perfect structure, but in faithful love that reflects Christ in the home. Ultimately, regardless of the family structure, Christ is the true head.

## Living Obedience Together

Holiness in family life is not built on constant agreement, but on mutual love lived out in daily actions. Respectful listening at the dinner table, finishing chores with patience, forgiving quickly after arguments, praying together even for a few minutes: these are the "Nazareth moments" where Christ dwells among us.

When families honor their roles (parents guiding with kindness, children responding with respect), Christ's peace takes root. This is not perfection, but holiness: the presence of God sanctifying ordinary life.

## Closing Prayer

> Heavenly Father,
> thank You for giving us the Holy Family as a
>     model of obedience, love, and unity.
> May Jesus inspire obedience,
> Mary guide us in faith,
> and Joseph strengthen us in responsibility.
> Make our homes places of peace and prayer,
> so that we may reflect Your love to the world.
> Amen.

## Reflection Questions

- How do the roles of Son, Mother, and Head in the Holy Family inspire my own family life?
- How do I show honor and respect to my parents, spouse, or children?
- What is one way I can practice immediate obedience or respectful listening this week?

## DAY 11

# The Holiness of Family Roles

*Jesus, Mary, and Joseph, divine child, pure spouse, and chaste spouse, pray for us.*

## Opening Scripture

"And the Word became flesh and dwelt among us, full of grace and truth; we have beheld his glory." *(John 1:14)*

## Hearts Reflecting God's Love

This line of the Litany highlights Jesus as the Divine Child, Mary as the Pure Spouse, and Joseph as the Chaste Spouse. These titles remind us that holiness is not revealed in worldly power, but in humility, self-giving love, and the grace that orders the human heart toward God. Each member of the Holy Family shows us a heart that reflects God's own: the Sacred Heart of Jesus, the Immaculate Heart of Mary, and the chaste, steadfast heart of Joseph.

## Jesus, the Divine Child

Though He is God's eternal Son, Jesus chose to enter the world as a true child: small, vulnerable, and dependent, sanctifying every stage of human life. In Nazareth, He grew in wisdom and obedience (Luke 2:51–52), teaching us that childhood itself is holy ground.

Devotion to the Sacred Heart of Jesus reminds us that His Heart, even as a child, was aflame with love for His Father and for us. His Heart burns with a love that never fades, a love constant, merciful, and unchanging. In a world where affection often wavers, the Sacred Heart assures us of God's steadfast presence: a love that is patient, faithful, and true in every season of life.

Jesus teaches the Beatitude: "Blessed are the pure in heart, for they shall see God" (Matthew 5:8). To be pure of heart is to see with the eyes of a child, with innocence, trust, and wonder. Catholic spirituality has always cherished this posture: to see God in prayer, in the Eucharist, and in the faces of those we love. The saints who lived this "little way," like St. Thérèse of Lisieux and the young saints Maria Goretti and Philomena, show that purity of heart is not naïve; it is grace made visible.

## Mary, the Pure Spouse

Mary's purity was more than virginity; it was the total consecration of her whole being to God. At the Annunciation she declared, "Behold, I am the handmaid of the Lord; let it be to me according to your word" (Luke 1:38). In that moment of complete surrender, she entrusted everything (her body, her future, her whole life) to God.

The Church venerates her Immaculate Heart as the perfect symbol of this undivided love: a heart entirely free from sin and open without reserve to God's will. For families today, Mary reminds us that purity is not fragility but strength. It is choosing to love with purity, honesty, and a whole heart, making of ourselves a gift for God and for others.

## Joseph, the Chaste Spouse

Joseph's love for Mary was marked by respect and sacrifice. He accepted God's plan for Mary's divine motherhood with trust, placing her welfare above his own. His chastity was not the absence of desire, but the perfection of love, expressed through service, reverence, and self-mastery.

In Christian art, Joseph is often depicted holding a lily, a symbol of purity and integrity of heart. His chaste love reveals that true strength lies in reverence, fidelity, and selfless devotion. For husbands, fathers, and guardians, Joseph teaches that headship means sacrificial love, a love that protects and serves rather than dominates. In Joseph's heart, strength and tenderness were one, a reflection of God's own fatherly love.

## Living Purity and Chastity at Home

In our home, we have enthroned the Sacred Heart of Jesus and the Immaculate Heart of Mary. Their images hang in a place of honor, a visible sign that Christ and His Mother reign at the center of our family life. Enthronement is a devotional act that helps families live more consciously within the grace of the Church's sacramental life. That visible reminder (Christ's Heart burning with steadfast love, and Mary's Heart completely given to God) keeps before us the kind of love we want to shape our family.

Teaching chastity in our home is more than a lesson about waiting for marriage; it is about forming the heart to love rightly. St. John Paul II's *Theology of the Body* reminds us that chastity is not simply "no" to sin, but a deeper "yes" to love, learning to treat others as gifts, not objects. For children, this virtue begins with small, daily choices: guarding their words, avoiding inappropriate entertainment, dressing modestly, and treating others as the gifts they truly are.

As Scripture says, "I appeal to you therefore, brethren, by the mercies of God, to present your bodies as a living sacrifice, holy and acceptable to God" (Romans 12:1). Teaching our children chastity means helping them see their bodies, their words, and their hearts as offerings of love, gifts they can freely give back to God. In the end, purity is not about what we avoid, but about who we are becoming: children with hearts ready to see God, just as Jesus promised in the Beatitudes, "Blessed are the pure in heart, for they shall see God" (Matthew 5:8).

## Closing Prayer

Heavenly Father,
we thank You for Jesus, the Divine Child,
Mary, the Pure Spouse,
and Joseph, the Chaste Spouse.
Help us live their virtues in our own families:
trust, purity, reverence, and self-giving love.
May our homes reflect the unity and holiness
of Nazareth.
Amen.

## Reflection Questions

- What does purity look like in my daily family relationships?
- How can I practice Joseph's selfless, chaste love in serving my family this week?
- Where is God inviting me to live with more childlike trust and purity of heart?

## DAY 12

## Restoring Hope at Home

*Jesus, Mary, and Joseph, restorers of fallen families, pray for us.*

## Opening Scripture

"With God all things are possible." *(Matthew 19:26)*

## Hope for Broken Families

Every family knows the weight of division: hurtful words, broken trust, or struggles that seem too heavy to carry. Yet no household is beyond God's reach. When we call the Holy Family "restorers of fallen families," we proclaim that grace can heal even the deepest wounds. How does that healing begin? Often in small, ordinary ways love is lived inside the home: in prayer, in forgiveness, and in the slow work of rebuilding trust.

The Catechism teaches that "children in turn contribute to the growth in holiness of their parents. Each and everyone should be generous and tireless in mutual affection and forgiveness" (CCC 2227). In other words, restoration unfolds not only through prayer but also through daily choices: to forgive, to love generously, and to walk together in humility. The Holy Family of Nazareth shows us that unity is not the absence of struggle, but the presence of love rooted in God, a love strong enough to transform what is broken.

## How the Holy Family Restores

Jesus, Mary, and Joseph restore fallen families not only by their intercession, but by the example of their lives.

- Jesus spent hidden years in Nazareth, teaching us that holiness grows in small, daily acts of love (Luke 2:51).
- Mary trusted God's plan even when a sword pierced her heart (Luke 2:35), showing that faith can endure through suffering.
- Joseph safeguarded his family during the flight into Egypt, revealing that sacrificial love protects and strengthens.

Together they teach that healing comes through prayer, humility, sacrifice, and trust in God. What looks ordinary (meals shared, work done faithfully, forgiveness offered quickly) becomes extraordinary when lived with love. Nazareth was a workshop of restoration, where holiness grew in the midst of daily life.

## Family Reflection

Fridays in my childhood meant a restaurant, a movie, or window-shopping. In our home, Fridays found a different rhythm: Confession night. Every week we pile into the car and head to our parish because we all need the grace of God, and we know it. "All have sinned and fall short of the glory of God" (Romans 3:23).

Why do we do this? Because we are a fallen family, and we need mercy. We have sprinted to the confessional five minutes before it closes, called out to each other as we scrambled out the door, and slipped into Mass a bit late more times than I can count. We've improved, but we still have messy days. Reconciliation has become a lifeline for us, the way God's mercy enters our home. Saturdays and Sundays feel lighter, more peaceful, after a good, honest confession.

I can say with confidence that the Holy Family has helped raise us through the sacraments. Jesus, Mary, and Joseph remind us that no family is beyond God's mercy. By their intercession (and through the grace of forgiveness, both received in the confessional and practiced at home), our fallen family is being restored, little by little, into something more like Nazareth: not perfect, but faithful, and striving toward perfection in love (Colossians 3:14).

## Healing in Our Families

Every family has "fallen places" that need God's mercy: grudges, disappointments, words we wish we could take back. Sometimes these wounds feel too old to mend or too deep to forgive. Yet even there, grace is stronger than sin. Restoration often begins not with sweeping change but with one small act of love: a kind word where there has been silence, a prayer for someone who has caused hurt, or a willingness to listen without judgment.

God multiplies small beginnings. Just as Nazareth was a place of hidden holiness, our homes can become places where quiet acts of forgiveness and patience bear great fruit. Families today can imitate Nazareth by setting aside time for daily prayer, choosing forgiveness instead of resentment (Matthew 18:21-22), and offering small acts of kindness even when emotions are strained. The Holy Family restores fallen families because they show us the way: prayer as refuge, the sacraments as strength, and virtue as the daily path to peace.

## The Help of the Saints

We are not alone in this work. The saints (and above all the Holy Family) walk with us and intercede for us. St. Monica prayed for years until Augustine's conversion, proving that no prayer for a loved one is wasted. Father Patrick Peyton, the Rosary Priest, reminded the world, "The family that prays together stays together." The saints' intercession participates in Christ's own intercession (Hebrews 7:25); their help never replaces His, but draws us more deeply into it.

When we invite the Holy Family and the saints into our struggles, we join the communion of love that binds the Church together. Their prayers strengthen ours, their example lights our way, and their witness gives us courage to keep moving forward in hope. When reconciliation seems impossible, they remind us that God can do what we cannot. When we grow weary of forgiving, they teach us to lean on grace. And when we feel alone, they assure us that heaven itself is invested in the healing of our families: "The Lord is near to the brokenhearted, and saves the crushed in spirit" (Psalm 34:18).

## Closing Prayer

> Jesus, Mary, and Joseph, restorers of fallen families,
> enter our homes.
> Heal our wounds, soften our hearts,
> and help us forgive one another.
> Teach us to trust God's mercy,
> so our families may be renewed in His love.
> Amen.

## Reflection Questions

- What "fallen" places in my family need God's healing grace?

- What one small step toward forgiveness or reconciliation can I take today?
- Do I truly believe no family is beyond God's mercy? How can I live that hope this week?

## DAY 13

# A Family That Reflects God

*Jesus, Mary, and Joseph, image of the Blessed Trinity here on earth, pray for us.*

## Opening Scripture

"Let us make man in our image, after our likeness... male and female he created them." *(Genesis 1:26–27)*

## The Family as an Image of the Trinity

When we pray this line of the Litany, we remember that every family bears the mark of its Creator. God is love, and within the Trinity (Father, Son, and Holy Spirit), that love is eternal, faithful, and life-giving. The Catechism teaches that the Christian family "is called to partake of the prayer and sacrifice of Christ" (CCC 2205) and becomes an image of the Trinity.

The Holy Family of Nazareth reflects this mystery on earth. They are not the Trinity itself, yet in their unity we glimpse heaven. Jesus shows obedience as the Son who does the will of the Father. Mary's openness to the Spirit shows the heart of receptivity and surrender. Joseph's steadfast care echoes the protective love of the Father. Each lived a unique mission, yet together they formed a communion of love, a living icon of divine life shared among loved ones.

## The Trinity in Daily Life

The hidden years of Nazareth were simple: Joseph's steady labor, Mary's prayerful presence, and Jesus' growth in wisdom and grace (Luke 2:51–52). Within those ordinary days, the eternal love of God was present. Their home was not merely a shelter but a reflection of heaven's communion.

St. Bernard of Clairvaux described the Trinity as a living exchange of love: the Father as the Lover, the Son as the Beloved, and the Holy Spirit as the Love that unites them. Love, for Bernard, is never static; it is ceaseless giving and receiving. The Holy Family mirrored that on earth: Joseph giving and protecting, Mary receiving and nurturing, and Jesus offering Himself in joyful obedience. Their home pulsed with that divine current of gratitude and self-gift.

St. Bonaventure called the Trinity the *fons plenitudinis* (fountain of fullness), a love so abundant that it cannot remain

# Day 13: A Family That Reflects God

enclosed but pours outward in creation and redemption. In the same way, divine love overflowed through the Holy Family into every act of their life in Nazareth. Christian families today are invited to let their love overflow beyond themselves through hospitality, compassion, and service.

When families live this mystery, daily routines become living echoes of the Trinity's harmony. Love that gives, love that receives, and love that overflows: this is the pattern written into the heart of God and into every family called to bear His image.

## Living as an Image of the Trinity

Families today reflect the Trinity by living unity in love. This does not mean every moment is peaceful, but that prayer, service, forgiveness, and charity form the fabric of life.

- Praying together keeps God at the center of the family.
- Serving one another with patience mirrors Christ's humility.
- Forgiving quickly heals division and protects unity.
- Loving sacrificially shows that charity is at the heart of family life.

In these ways, our homes become small reflections of God's eternal love, proclaiming with every act that "God is love" (1 John 4:8).

## Family Reflection

When I think about the birth of each of our children, I see how God's love expands the heart. For many years it was just my husband and me, and we sometimes wondered whether our love, before children, still reflected the Holy Trinity. The answer is yes. The image of divine love is not measured by numbers in a household but by the love shared within it.

Even before Jesus was born, Mary and Joseph lived this mystery. Their virginal, chaste love was a perfect image of Trinitarian harmony: faithful, self-giving, and open to God's will. Though they had no physical union, their relationship was fruitful in holiness: through the overshadowing of the Holy Spirit and Mary's *fiat*, the Word of God entered the world. Chosen by divine providence, Joseph embraced his vocation with obedient faith, serving as the guardian of the Redeemer and the protector of the Virgin. Their example reminds every family that true love, purified and directed toward God, always gives life through prayer, service, compassion, or spiritual motherhood and fatherhood.

In the same way, couples who long for children but cannot conceive, families who have lost little ones, and guardians raising children not their own also bear this divine image. In Catholic teaching, fruitfulness is not only biological but spiritual. The Catechism teaches that "spouses share in the creative power and fatherhood of God" (CCC 372) and that this fruitfulness includes "the moral and spiritual education" and care of others (CCC 1653). Every act of love that participates in God's self-giving (nurturing a child, comforting a friend, mentoring, or caring for the suffering) reflects the inner life of the Trinity.

# Day 13: A Family That Reflects God

The birth of our children deepened our sense of that divine love. With each new life entrusted to us, I felt God drawing our family into His order of giving and receiving, the same pattern that exists among Father, Son, and Holy Spirit. Yet even before our home was full of children, the image of the Trinity was already there: love that gives, love that receives, and love that unites. That is the mystery of Nazareth and the promise for every family, whatever its form.

## Closing Prayer

> Triune God,
> through Jesus, Mary, and Joseph,
> You have shown that heaven's love can dwell in
>     an earthly home.
> Consecrate our family in Your image.
> Make our words truthful, our work generous,
>     and our love steadfast.
> May all who enter our home glimpse the light
>     of Your communion.
> Amen.

## Reflection Questions

- How does the Holy Family help me understand the love of the Trinity?
- In what moments has my family reflected unity in love?
- What is one step we can take this week to live more like the Trinity in our home?

## DAY 14

# Faith in the Midst of Trials

*Holy Family, tested by the greatest
of difficulties, pray for us.*

## Opening Scripture

"Count it all joy, my brethren, when you meet various trials, for you know that the testing of your faith produces steadfastness." *(James 1:2-3)*

## Faith Tested in Fire

The Holy Family is honored in the Litany as those "tested by the greatest of difficulties." Their story was marked by hardship from the beginning: an unexpected pregnancy, misunderstanding, poverty, exile, and the looming sorrow of the Cross. Yet in every trial, Jesus, Mary, and Joseph remained faithful, humble, and trusting in God.

The Catechism teaches that "faith is often lived in darkness and can be put to the test" (CCC 164). Faith that endures hardship is refined like gold in fire. The Holy Family shows us that trials are not signs of God's absence but invitations to draw closer to Him. Nazareth was not a haven from pain but a home sanctified by love, a school where patience, forgiveness, and trust were practiced daily.

Their example reveals that holiness grows in the soil of difficulty. Joseph bore anxiety quietly, Mary held sorrow in her heart, and Jesus "learned obedience through what he suffered" (Hebrews 5:8). Through it all, divine love and the desire to do God's will bound them together. The same grace that strengthened them is offered to every family that cries out to God in hardship.

## Lessons for Our Families

The Holy Family faced suffering not with despair but with surrender. Each responded to trial with virtue:

- **Mary's yes in fear:** At the Annunciation, she risked misunderstanding and rejection, yet her "yes" teaches us to trust God when the future feels uncertain (Luke 1:38).
- **Joseph's obedience in crisis:** Faced with confusion, he chose compassion and listened to God's guidance (Mat-

thew 1:24). His example teaches us to respond with mercy and trust when conflicts arise.
- **Jesus' suffering and the Cross:** Mary's presence at Calvary reminds us that no sorrow is wasted when joined to Christ.

The Catechism reminds us that "the cross is the unique sacrifice of Christ, the mediator between God and men," yet we are called to take up our own crosses and share in His redemptive love (CCC 618). When we unite our suffering with His, pain becomes a channel of grace for ourselves and for those we love.

## The Witness of Louis and Zélie Martin

Few couples reflect this truth more clearly than Saints Louis and Zélie Martin, the parents of St. Thérèse of Lisieux. Their marriage was marked by deep love and profound suffering. Zélie faced her illness and offered her pain in union with Christ, writing, "When I think of all I have to suffer, I bless God, and I am full of joy." Louis, too, bore his cross in his later years when his health declined. Even then he radiated peace and trust, often whispering, "I want whatever He wants." Their home became a crucible of redemptive love. From that fidelity amid suffering came extraordinary fruit: five daughters in religious life, among them a Doctor of the Church. The Martins show that suffering, united to the Cross, bears tremendous spiritual fruit.

## Family Reflection

Our family, like every family, has known trials. There were seasons when uncertainty seemed to shadow every day: sudden job loss, financial strain, and moves that left us feeling like nomads searching for stability. In those moments, I often thought of the Holy Family (Joseph leading Mary and the Child Jesus from Nazareth to Bethlehem, into exile in Egypt, and back again). They knew what it was like to live between places and to trust God when tomorrow was unclear. Those years tested our faith in ways we could not have anticipated; looking back, I see how God was forming us through those hardships, teaching us dependence on His providence and compassion for others in similar need.

When disappointments, arguments, setbacks, illness, or painful separations arise, we remind our children to unite them to the Cross. We tell them, "The Cross is the place of Jesus' greatest intercession." When we bring our pain and helplessness there, it is no longer meaningless; it becomes powerful.

Padre Pio taught that in heaven we would look back on our sufferings with joy, seeing how they helped us grow in holiness. I try to instill that truth: that suffering is not useless, but suffused with God's power when offered in love. The Holy Family also knew insecurity and uncertainty (Mary and Joseph fleeing into Egypt without knowing where they would rest; Jesus, carrying His Cross, misunderstood and alone). Suffering is not a sign of God's absence but the place of His deepest work. When I see my children beginning to unite their struggles (big or small) to Christ's Cross, I recognize the quiet fruit of those difficult years.

God was not abandoning us; He was teaching us to trust Him more deeply and showing our family that every hardship can become a prayer.

## Living This Trust Today

Families grow stronger in trials when they turn to God together. Testing purifies faith, and love refined by suffering becomes steadfast and merciful. When life feels uncertain or painful, the Holy Family stands beside us as witnesses that holiness is forged through perseverance.

We can live this trust in simple ways:

- Pray together daily, especially in seasons of stress or uncertainty.
- Choose simplicity: let go of what is not essential and be grateful for what remains.
- Forgive quickly when tension rises, following Joseph's example of mercy.
- Support others who suffer; reach out to neighbors, friends, or strangers with concrete care.
- Repeat often: "Jesus, I trust in You." Drawn from the message of Divine Mercy, this short prayer becomes a heartbeat of faith.

God does not waste pain; He transforms it. When families place their wounds in His hands, even sorrow becomes sacred.

## Closing Prayer

> Holy Family,
> tested by hardships greater than our own, pray
>     for us in our trials.
> Help us to remain faithful,
> to forgive generously,
> and to walk in hope when the way is hard.
> May our families be strengthened by your
>     example
> and renewed by the power of Christ's Cross.
> Amen.

## Reflection Questions

- What trial in my family life has tested my faith the most?
- How do Mary and Joseph's responses to hardship inspire me?
- How can my family turn trials into opportunities for prayer, love, and unity this week?

WEEK 3

# The Humility of Bethlehem

## DAY 15

## The Road to Bethlehem

*Holy Family, with much suffering on the journey to Bethlehem, pray for us.*

## Opening Scripture

"Blessed are those whose strength is in You, in whose heart are the highways to Zion. As they go through the valley of tears, they make it a place of springs." *(Psalm 84:5-7)*

## The Journey of Faith

The road to Bethlehem was not the peaceful procession we often imagine. Mary neared the end of pregnancy, Joseph bore the weight of responsibility, and the path stretched mile after mile in uncertainty. Yet they walked in trust, knowing that God's plan was unfolding even in hardship.

Like the psalmist's pilgrims, the Holy Family passed through valleys of weariness and tears, but their faith transformed the journey into grace. Their perseverance teaches that holiness often grows precisely in the moments that test us most. God's strength is made perfect in weakness, and the road that feels desolate can become, in His providence, a place of blessing.

The Catechism reminds us that fortitude enables us to remain firm in difficulties and constant in the pursuit of the good (CCC 1808). The Holy Family's perseverance shows what this virtue looks like in daily life. Their suffering on the road teaches that grace does not always remove hardship but transforms it into a pathway toward deeper faith.

St. John Paul II taught that in the family of Nazareth, faith is born anew under the gaze of the Holy Family, and it is this faith which shows the Church how to continue to share in the mystery of the Incarnation (Redemptoris Custos, 6). What appeared to be a weary journey was, in truth, the unfolding of salvation. The same is true for our families. God often leads us through difficulty so that trust might take root and love might mature.

## Lessons for Families

- **Mary's Example:** Though tired and vulnerable, Mary kept her heart fixed on God's promise. She invites us to

surrender our fears and believe that God can bring blessing even in discomfort.
- **Joseph's Example:** As protector and guide, Joseph carried responsibility with quiet strength. His fidelity in silence reminds us that love is proven more by endurance than by words.
- **The Stable in Bethlehem:** Turned away from every door, they found shelter in humility. Yet there, heaven touched earth. The manger became the first altar where the Bread of Life was first laid, and the poverty of Bethlehem became the sign of God's abundance.

Their story reminds us that holiness is not dependent on comfort or certainty but on trust. God's will may lead us down unfamiliar roads, yet He never abandons those who walk with Him in faith.

## The Bethlehem Spirit in Every Home

The journey to Bethlehem is repeated in every generation. Families still walk roads marked by fatigue, transition, and waiting. Financial strain, illness, or uncertainty about the future can make us feel like strangers in our own land. Yet Bethlehem teaches that every hardship can become sacred ground when lived with love and faith.

St. Francis of Assisi saw this clearly. Captivated by the humility of the Nativity, he created the first live crèche so others could see and touch the mystery of God made poor for love of us. For Francis, Bethlehem was not a memory but a daily attitude: a readiness to welcome Christ in simplicity and joy.

When our families choose gratitude instead of complaint, generosity instead of fear, and prayer instead of worry, we too make room for Jesus in the inn of our hearts.

## Family Reflection

Not long after our first child was born, our little family packed up everything we owned (including a few bewildered cats) and set off on a cross-country move so my husband could pursue graduate studies in theology. Picture it: two adults, a one-year-old, and four cats in a car so small that every inch of space was spoken for. It felt less like a road trip and more like a pilgrimage on wheels, a tiny caravan inching north, state after state, mile after mile.

Were we a little crazy? Probably. But looking back, I see that same seed of faith that moved Mary and Joseph to set out for Bethlehem. Like them, we didn't know exactly what waited at the end of the road. The long hours were uncomfortable, the car was hot and cramped, and we carried more uncertainty than luggage. Yet beneath it all was joy, the joy that comes from saying yes to God's will, even when it looks absurd from the outside.

The Church Fathers often spoke of the journey to Bethlehem as obedience in motion: love walking forward in faith. They reflected that in the hardships surrounding Christ's birth, Mary and Joseph displayed perfect trust in God, a faith through which the hope of the world entered history. Mary and Joseph's weariness was great, but greater still was their trust, for they bore not only their own burdens but the hope of the world. Their perseverance sanctified every rough mile of that dusty road.

In our own small way, that long drive became our Bethlehem journey. There were moments of weariness and frustration, but also laughter, grace, and peace in knowing we were exactly where God wanted us. The car became our little Nazareth: cramped, imperfect, but filled with love and a quiet sense of mission.

Just as God entered the world in a stable, He enters our lives in humble, uncomfortable moments, in places we least expect Him. That trip taught me that holiness often begins in the ordinary journey, when we choose to move forward with trust and a heart ready to do God's will, even when it makes no sense to anyone else.

## Living the Lesson Today

Every family has its own Bethlehem road, seasons when we carry heavy burdens and see no clear destination. Like Mary and Joseph, we can take the next step in faith, confident that God will meet us along the way. To nurture this spirit of faith, as a family:

- Pray together during stressful or uncertain times, asking God to guide each step.
- Embrace simplicity, remembering that holiness often grows in hidden and humble places.
- Offer each day's fatigue or inconvenience for someone who is suffering more.

- Make space for Christ: a candle lit, a prayer whispered, a word of kindness offered. All become spiritual mangers where He can dwell.

Bethlehem teaches that God's greatest miracles often begin in obscurity. When families walk their journeys with faith and perseverance, the light of Christ shines through their trust.

## Closing Prayer

> Jesus, Mary, and Joseph,
> You endured suffering on the way to
>    Bethlehem.
> Strengthen us in our own trials.
> Teach us to walk with courage, to support one
>    another with love,
> and to trust God's providence at every step.
> Amen.

## Reflection Questions

- What "Bethlehem journeys" has my family faced recently?
- How do Mary and Joseph's trust in hardship inspire me?
- What small act of perseverance or faith can I practice this week?

## DAY 16

# Finding God in Rejection

*Holy Family, without a welcome
in Bethlehem, pray for us.*

## Opening Scripture

"She gave birth to her firstborn son and wrapped him in swaddling cloths and laid him in a manger, because there was no room for them in the inn." *(Luke 2:7)*

## No Room at the Inn

When Mary and Joseph arrived in Bethlehem, weary and expectant, they found closed doors. There was "no room" for them. In that rejection, the Son of God was born not in comfort but in a stable.

This moment is more than history; it is a mirror of the human heart. Just as Bethlehem's inns were too full, our lives can also become crowded with worry, ambition, distraction, or self-reliance. Christ does not force His way in; He comes quietly, knocking. He found no room in the inn on earth, so that He might prepare for us many mansions in heaven. In every generation, the question remains: will there be room for Him?

## Lessons from Mary and Joseph

- **Mary's Trust:** Vulnerable and great with child, Mary accepted the humility of giving birth in poor surroundings. She shows that surrender to God's will, even in disappointment, leads to peace.
- **Joseph's Faithfulness:** Faced with rejection and uncertainty, Joseph remained steadfast. His silent strength teaches that love often speaks most powerfully in action.
- **The Stable's Message:** God's glory appeared in the most unexpected of places, teaching that His love can transform even hidden or painful circumstances into channels of grace.

St. John Chrysostom observed that while kings sought palaces, Christ found His throne in a manger. The lowliness of His birth is not accidental; it is God's way of drawing near to the lowly.

# Day 16: Finding God in Rejection

## A World That Still Closes Its Doors

The story of Bethlehem continues in every generation. Families today face their own "closed doors": rejection, financial hardship, illness, loneliness, or misunderstanding. Sometimes even faith itself meets resistance in hearts grown weary or skeptical. Yet the Holy Family teaches that holiness is not the absence of hardship but faith in God's presence within it.

Bethlehem's poverty became God's glory. When our homes feel too small, our plans uncertain, or our efforts overlooked, we are closer to the manger than we realize. The stable of Bethlehem proves that love needs no luxury, only a heart open to receive it.

## Family Reflection

There was a time when our family seemed to encounter one closed door after another. We had moved more times than I could count. During one difficult season, we found ourselves without a stable home, depending on promises of help that never came. Each time hope seemed within reach, it was withdrawn, and we were left trying to discern what God wanted of us next.

We were about to welcome a new baby, and the days were long and uncertain. I remember the exhaustion and disappointment, yet even in that darkness, a small light of faith remained. We chose to trust that, somehow, God would provide, that if He had brought us this far, He would not abandon us now.

When we finally left that situation behind, not knowing what awaited us, God sent help in an unexpected way. Friends from our parish learned what was happening and opened their home to us. In that act of kindness, I saw the mercy of God, the same mercy that found the Holy Family shelter in a stable when no one else would take them in.

Like Mary and Joseph in Bethlehem, we learned that rejection is not the end of the story. Sometimes it is the beginning of God's greater plan, a plan that teaches us to see His providence more clearly and His people more tenderly. The absence of welcome in one place can make room for grace to appear in another.

## Living This Today

Each day offers moments to open or close the door of our hearts to Christ. The Holy Family shows that even in rejection, God's plan unfolds with purpose. When we welcome others (especially those who are lonely, struggling, or overlooked), we welcome Christ Himself.

**To "make room" for Jesus this week:**

- Begin each day with prayer, asking God to make your heart a dwelling for His peace.
- Practice hospitality, even in small ways: welcome the stranger, listen with compassion, include the overlooked.
- Let go of distractions that crowd out prayer; even a few minutes of silence can open wide the door of the soul.

# Day 16: Finding God in Rejection

As we open our homes and hearts to God's presence, the same light that filled the stable of Bethlehem can fill our families with peace.

## Closing Prayer

Jesus, Mary, and Joseph,
you found no welcome in Bethlehem,
yet you welcomed the world with God's love.
Help us make room in our hearts and homes
   for Christ.
Teach us to trust God in rejection,
to welcome the forgotten,
and to live with hope when doors seem closed.
Amen.

## Reflection Questions

- What "closed doors" has my family faced, and how did God still provide?
- What distractions crowd out space for Christ in my heart?
- How can we practice hospitality and welcome in our home this week?

# DAY 17

# God Reveals Himself to the Lowly

*Holy Family, visited by the poor shepherds, pray for us.*

## Opening Scripture

"And they went with haste and found Mary and Joseph, and the baby lying in a manger." *(Luke 2:16)*

## The Humble Who See God

When the angels announced Christ's birth, the first to hear were not kings or scholars but poor shepherds keeping watch in the fields. Considered outsiders, they were chosen to receive the "good news of great joy" (Luke 2:10). In their eagerness to go "with haste" to the manger, they teach that God's love is not reserved for the powerful or the worthy, but is revealed to the humble and ready of heart.

The Catechism reminds us: "Jesus was born in a humble stable, into a poor family. Simple shepherds were the first witnesses to this event. In this poverty heaven's glory was made manifest" (CCC 525). From His first moments on earth, Christ overturned worldly expectations. The weary and unpolished shepherds became the first evangelists, returning to their fields "glorifying and praising God" (Luke 2:20).

The Holy Family's welcome of the shepherds reflected the generosity of God Himself. Though Mary and Joseph had little to offer, they made room for others. Their warmth shows that love is not measured by possessions but by presence. As St. Gregory the Great teaches, the message of Christ's birth was revealed to humble shepherds, reminding us that God delights to make His glory known to the simple of heart (Homilies on the Gospels, 8). Holiness, like light, often begins in lowly places.

## Lessons for Families

- **The Shepherds' Joy:** They left everything to seek the newborn Christ. Families, too, are called to make Jesus their first priority, to run "with haste" toward prayer, worship, and service.
- **Mary's Contemplation:** Mary "treasured up all these things and pondered them in her heart" (Luke 2:19). Her quiet reflection balances the shepherds' zeal, showing that faith is both active and contemplative.

- **Joseph's Hospitality:** Joseph created a humble space where the poor were welcomed. His example reminds families that love always finds room for others, even when resources or energy are limited.

Together the shepherds and the Holy Family show that joy and humility belong together. The first Christmas gathering was not among royalty but among the poor, the faithful, and the open-hearted.

## The Manger: God's Open Door

The manger is the answer to every "no room" in Bethlehem. Where the world closed its doors, God opened His arms. The stable became a place of welcome for shepherds and, later, for wise men from afar, a sign that divine mercy knows no boundaries.

Christ's first visitors were the poor; His last act on earth was to forgive the thief on the cross. The pattern is the same: grace begins with those who know their need for Him. Pope Leo XIV reminds us that "the gravest poverty is not to know God," and that the poor "are not a distraction for the Church but our beloved brothers and sisters." In this encounter, we are placed face-to-face with the truth of the Gospel.

Our homes, too, can become mangers of mercy, places where others find warmth, listening, support, and love. When we welcome the poor and forgotten, we make space for Christ Himself.

## Family Reflection

During Advent, I often meditate on the Holy Family and the Nativity scene. The moment when heaven bends low to earth never loses its wonder: "And the Word became flesh and dwelt among us, full of grace and truth" (John 1:14).

I imagine the flicker of lamplight on rough beams, the scent of hay, the sound of animals, and the shepherds entering quietly, their clothes still smelling of the fields. The stable was simple, perhaps uncomfortable, yet within it heaven touched earth.

In prayer I sometimes ask, "Lord, in this Nativity scene, who am I?" Following the tradition of St. Ignatius of Loyola, I place myself in the Gospel story. In my heart I sense that I am one of the poor shepherds. At first the thought surprises me, then fills me with peace.

The shepherds were poor in goods but rich in what matters most: openness, humility, readiness to respond. When the angels spoke, they left everything and went "with haste" to find the Child. Their work, possessions, and weariness faded before the joy of seeing Jesus. That is the posture God desires: a heart willing to leave behind whatever hinders His presence.

In prayer I realize that Jesus is pleased when we come as the shepherds: simple, unpolished, sincere. He invites us to approach without fear or pretense, bringing nothing but longing and love. Each time we do, we become witnesses of the same miracle: Christ welcomed into the poverty of the human heart.

# Day 17: God Reveals Himself to the Lowly

## Living the Message Today

The shepherds remind us that faith begins with wonder and humility. God still seeks the lowly places of our world and our hearts to reveal His presence.

To live this spirit as a family:

- **Welcome others:** Invite someone who might feel left out into your home or your prayer.
- **Teach empathy:** Help children notice those who seem lonely and reach out with kindness.
- **Serve together:** Share a meal, volunteer, or send encouragement to someone in need.
- **Reflect like Mary:** End the day with quiet gratitude, "pondering in your heart" how God has shown Himself that day.

When we make room for the poor, the lonely, and the forgotten, we welcome Christ Himself, and the joy of Bethlehem fills our homes anew.

## Closing Prayer

> Holy Family,
> who welcomed the poor shepherds at Bethlehem,

teach us to see Christ in the lowly.
Give us hearts open to the poor, hands that
    serve with love,
and voices that proclaim the good news with
    joy.
Amen.

## Reflection Questions

- Why do you think God chose the poor shepherds to hear the angels' message first?
- Who in my life might be like those shepherds: overlooked, yet precious to God?
- How can my family welcome Christ by welcoming others this week?

## DAY 18

# God's Presence in Poverty

*Holy Family, obliged to live in a stable, pray for us.*

## Opening Scripture

"For you know the grace of our Lord Jesus Christ, that though he was rich, yet for your sake he became poor, so that by his poverty you might become rich." *(2 Corinthians 8:9)*

## God in the Stable

When Mary and Joseph found no room at the inn, they accepted the only shelter left: a stable. It was poor, hidden, and uncomfortable, yet it became the place where the Savior of the world entered history.

St. Gregory Nazianzen reflected on this divine humility: "He who is rich is made poor; He takes on the poverty of my flesh, that I may gain the riches of His divinity" (Oration 45, On Holy Pascha). In the cold stillness of that night, the Creator of the stars lay beneath them, wrapped not in majesty but in swaddling cloths. The stable of Bethlehem is the place of this sacred exchange, where heaven stoops low so that humanity might be lifted high.

The stable teaches that no circumstance is too small or too humble for divine love to dwell. The same God who filled that poor shelter with His glory still enters the simplest homes and the most ordinary lives. Holiness does not depend on comfort, but on openness to grace. Even the roughest corners of our lives can become Bethlehem when we welcome Him there.

## Lessons from the Stable

- **Mary's Trust:** Giving birth in such conditions was far from ideal, yet Mary's heart remained surrendered to God's plan. Her Magnificat reminds us that "He has lifted up the lowly" (Luke 1:52). She teaches that peace is found not in control, but in confidence that God is near.
- **Joseph's Faithfulness:** Though he surely desired better for his family, Joseph remained steady and protective. His quiet obedience shows that love perseveres even when plans fall apart.

- **The Manger's Message:** Laid in a feeding trough, the newborn Christ foreshadows the Bread of Life given to us in the Eucharist. The manger (a place for food) becomes a prophetic image of the altar. God transforms the simplest spaces into signs of His saving love.

The stable of Bethlehem invites us to see our homes, however small or imperfect, as places where Christ desires to dwell.

## The Hidden Glory of the Stable

The world saw a poor couple in an animal shelter; heaven saw the King of Glory enthroned among straw. The humility of the Incarnation reveals that God's greatness is measured not by splendor but by love.

St. Ambrose marveled at this mystery: "He was a baby and a child, so that you may be a perfect man; He was wrapped in swaddling clothes, that you may be loosed from the snares of death; He was on earth, that you may be in heaven" (Exposition of the Gospel of Luke, 2.41). The Lord of glory chose weakness and poverty to free us from the fear of suffering and death.

In the stable, Mary and Joseph teach us to release what we think life should be and to receive what God gives with gratitude. The very hardships that seemed like obstacles became part of divine providence. The cold, the straw, and the silence were all transformed by the warmth of love.

Sometimes, when I'm driving through town, I notice a man who sits at the junction where three roads meet. Day after day, in heat or cold, he sits quietly with a cardboard sign, asking for help. I don't know his story (where he lives, whether anyone knows his name), but I often find myself thinking about him long after I pass. I drive home and wonder: where does he go? Does he have blankets, food, a roof over his head? I think of how the Holy Family, too, had no home that night, how they borrowed shelter meant for animals, a space that belonged to no one. The Son of God entered the world as a guest, dependent on the kindness of others, sanctifying every place where the poor must rest.

This man reminds me of Bethlehem: unnoticed by most, sitting at the crossroads of hurried lives, yet silently revealing something of Christ's poverty. The stable was not grand; it was simple and exposed to the elements. Yet that was where the Savior chose to dwell. I wonder if God still waits for us in such places, on the margins, where poverty meets the road and love has the chance to stop, to see, and to recognize Him.

Perhaps that is Bethlehem's invitation: to pause long enough to notice Christ hidden in the ordinary and the overlooked, and to make room for Him not only in our hearts, but in our compassion. As St. Mother Teresa of Calcutta said, Jesus comes to us "in His most distressing disguise," hidden in the poor, the lonely, and the forgotten, waiting for us to recognize and love Him there.

## Living the Stable Today

Families can take the stable as a call to simplicity and hospitality. The Holy Family shows that holiness is not found in wealth or status, but in love that sanctifies the ordinary.

## Day 18: God's Presence in Poverty

**Ways to live this spirit of simplicity:**

- Practice gratitude instead of complaint when life feels cramped or difficult.
- Create space for others, especially those who feel forgotten or out of place.
- Simplify possessions and priorities, freeing your home and heart for what truly matters.
- Find God in small moments: shared meals, quiet prayer, laughter, and care for one another.

God's presence transforms every humble dwelling into a Bethlehem. When we make peace with simplicity, we discover that joy has already taken root in our midst.

## Closing Prayer

> Jesus, Mary, and Joseph, who found shelter in
>   a stable,
> teach us to welcome God in humble places.
> Help us to embrace simplicity, to serve with
>   generosity,
> and to trust that Christ's presence
> can transform even our hardships into grace.
> Amen.

## Reflection Questions

- What "stable" places in my life feel too poor or unworthy for God's presence?
- How does the humility of Christ's birth challenge my attachment to comfort or status?
- What practical step can my family take this week to live with greater simplicity and welcome?

# DAY 19

# Heaven Rejoices on Earth

*Holy Family, praised by the angels, pray for us.*

## Opening Scripture

"Glory to God in the highest, and on earth peace among those with whom He is pleased." *(Luke 2:14)*

## The Song of Heaven

On that first Christmas night, quiet fields were suddenly ablaze with light and song. A multitude of angels proclaimed the birth of Christ, praising God and announcing peace on earth. At the center of it all was the Holy Family: a young mother, a faithful guardian, and a newborn Child, surrounded not by earthly acclaim but by heaven's joy.

Mary held the Child, Joseph kept watch, and the angels sang. Their hymn reveals that even the humblest places become radiant when Christ is present.

The Catechism teaches: "From the Incarnation to the Ascension, the life of the Word incarnate is surrounded by the adoration and service of angels" (CCC 333). The Nativity was not only the dawn of salvation for humanity, but also a moment of worship for heaven itself. The angels' cry ("Glory to God in the highest") is the Church's first Christmas carol and still resounds every time we sing the Gloria at Mass. When we lift our voices in that hymn, we stand beside the shepherds, Mary, and Joseph, joining the worship of heaven.

St. Gregory the Great taught that the angels sing not for God's sake but for ours, so that we might learn to praise. Their song is an invitation. Each time we turn our hearts to gratitude or lift our voices in prayer, we join their chorus of eternal joy.

## Lessons from Mary and Joseph

- **Mary's Contemplation:** Luke tells us she "kept all these things, pondering them in her heart" (Luke 2:19). While the shepherds hurried to share the good news, Mary teaches us the other half of worship: to treasure God's mysteries quietly, letting them sink deep into the soul.
- **Joseph's Silent Faith:** Joseph heard God's voice in dreams and obeyed. His faith, steady and hidden, harmonized with heaven's praise in an equally powerful way. His silence was not absence but awe.

Together, Mary and Joseph show us that heaven's joy and human faithfulness belong side by side. The angels' song echoes most clearly in hearts that listen, obey, and adore.

## Heaven's Music in Ordinary Life

The hymn of the angels still resounds through time, meant to be lived as much as sung. Every time a parent comforts a child, a family prays together, or forgiveness is offered, heaven's melody is heard again on earth.

The early Church Fathers saw this mystery clearly. St. Augustine explained that the angels' song of "peace to men of good will" refers to those who receive the gift of grace. Peace is not merely the absence of conflict but the harmony of hearts that live according to God's will. When love reigns in a family, that harmony becomes a foretaste of heaven's music.

At Christmas (and in every season), the Holy Family reminds us that praise and peace belong together. Worship transforms the ordinary: a home filled with laughter, a quiet act of service, a whispered prayer before the Nativity. These are the carols heaven hears most clearly.

## Family Reflection

Every Christmas Eve at Mass, I am moved to tears during the Gloria. As the choir begins, "Glory to God in the highest, and on earth peace to people of good will," I whisper to myself: we are singing the same song the angels sang to Christ on the night He was born.

In that moment, time seems to fold. Bethlehem feels close, and heaven seems near. I look at my husband and children beside me, their voices mingling with the congregation, and I realize we are all singing with the angels. The same hymn that once filled the skies above the shepherds now rises from the hearts of believers around the world, at every Christmas, every Mass, every act of praise.

Tears always come, tears of awe and gratitude. It feels as if the veil between heaven and earth lifts for a moment, and I can sense what the shepherds must have felt: fear giving way to wonder, silence breaking into joy. The Gloria reminds me that the Incarnation is not only remembered but entered.

Christmas worship gives us a glimpse of what the angels see unceasingly: the glory of God made flesh, love dwelling among us. Their song continues, and when we lift our voices in faith and love, we join their eternal chorus. Those tears are not sadness, but heaven's joy finding a home in the human heart.

## To live heaven's hymn as a family:

- Pray the Gloria at Mass with renewed awareness. You echo the angels of Bethlehem.
- Pause in gratitude: before meals or at day's end, give thanks aloud as a family.
- Keep peace at home: choose words that build up, forgive quickly, and create harmony.
- Lift others in joy: a smile, a note, or a visit to someone lonely becomes a verse in heaven's song.

The angels' hymn is not a relic of Christmas night; it is the rhythm of a life lived in praise. When we choose gratitude over grumbling, love over indifference, and faith over fear, the refrain begins again: "Glory to God in the highest, and on earth peace."

## Closing Prayer

> Holy Family,
> praised by the angels of heaven,
> teach us to lift our hearts in adoration.
> Help us to live with gratitude,
> to make our homes places of peace,
> and to echo heaven's hymn in our daily lives.
> Amen.

## Reflection Questions

- How do I join in the angels' praise in my daily life?
- What does Mary's example of pondering teach me about prayer?
- How can my family become a place where "Glory to God in the highest" is lived out in love and peace?

# DAY 20

---

# The Visit of the Magi

*Holy Family, venerated by the wise men from the East, pray for us.*

## Opening Scripture

"On entering the house, they saw the child with Mary his mother; and they knelt down and paid him homage. Then, opening their treasures, they offered him gifts of gold, frankincense, and myrrh." *(Matthew 2:11)*

## The Adoration of the Wise Men

The story of the Magi is one of faith, wonder, and revelation. Guided by a star and a longing for truth, they traveled from distant lands to bow before a Child in humble surroundings. They remind us that Christ came not for one people alone but for the whole world. Every heart, no matter how far it begins, is invited to seek and find Him.

The Catechism teaches: "The Epiphany is the manifestation of Jesus as Messiah of Israel, Son of God and Savior of the world. In the Magi, the representatives of neighboring pagan religions, the Gospel sees the first-fruits of the nations who welcome the good news of salvation through the Incarnation" (CCC 528).

St. Leo the Great expressed that in the persons of the Magi, we should recognize the first-fruits of our calling and of our faith (Sermo 31, De Epiphania Domini). The Magi kneel before Christ on behalf of all who will one day believe; their adoration is the beginning of our own.

Their gifts carry meaning that reaches across time:

- Gold honors Jesus as King.
- Frankincense acknowledges His divinity.
- Myrrh foreshadows His suffering and redeeming love.

St. Gregory the Great reflected, "They adored in that little one whom they saw, the God whom they did not see" (Hom. 10 in Evang. 6). In their worship, heaven and earth met in a simple home at Bethlehem, a reminder that God's glory often hides in simplicity and that every Eucharist renews this same adoration.

## Lessons for Families

- **Mary's Welcome:** Matthew tells us that the Magi "found the Child with Mary His mother." Her pres-

ence turns their homage into hospitality. She teaches us to receive others with reverence, patience, and openness.
- **Joseph's Protection:** Joseph safeguarded this sacred encounter, offering quiet strength and security. His fidelity reminds parents and guardians that love protects and shelters holiness.
- **Our Response:** Like the Magi, families are called to bring gifts to Christ, not gold or incense, but the treasures of love, patience, forgiveness, and time. These are offerings that please Him most.

Every act of service, every moment of mercy, every prayer whispered in trust becomes a gift laid before the King.

## Family Reflection

The visit of the Magi reveals one of faith's most beautiful truths: Jesus came not only for one nation but for all. The Magi were Gentiles, seekers from distant lands and unfamiliar traditions. In Scripture, "Gentiles" often described those who did not yet know the God of Israel. Yet they were drawn by grace, guided by a star, and found themselves kneeling before the Savior of the world.

Their story reminds us that God's call reaches far beyond our families, parishes, or culture. In them we see the prophecy fulfilled: "Nations shall come to your light, and kings to the brightness of your rising" (Isaiah 60:3). The Magi are a sign of hope for all who still search for God, for those who have not yet believed, who have drifted, or who feel unworthy to approach Him.

At Easter, the Church prays "for those who do not yet believe in God," asking that they may know the joy of salvation. Christmas and Easter meet here: the Child of Bethlehem is the Crucified and Risen Lord who redeems every heart. The cradle and the cross form one mission of mercy, to bring all people into the light of divine love.

As a family, we try to remember this by praying for those in our lives who do not yet know God: relatives, friends, or neighbors who have turned away from faith or never encountered it. Faith is not a possession but a gift meant to be shared. Jesus came, as He said, "not to call the righteous, but sinners" (Mark 2:17). The Magi show what that invitation looks like: strangers welcomed, outsiders drawn close, hearts once distant now adoring.

Their gifts tell this story, too:

- Gold proclaims the kingship of Christ over every nation and heart.
- Frankincense symbolizes the prayer of all peoples rising before God.
- Myrrh foreshadows the sacrifice that will redeem the world.

Each time we look upon the Nativity and see the Magi kneeling beside the manger, we are invited to pray for those still on their journey, for seekers and doubters, for the weary and the lost. The star still shines, and the Child still waits to receive the gifts of every heart.

## Living the Magi's Example

The Magi teach that faith is both a journey and an offering. Their story calls us to seek Christ with perseverance and to give Him our best.

**Ways to live this spirit as a family:**

- **Offer your treasures:** give time, kindness, and talent in service to others.
- **Seek Christ daily:** follow His light through prayer and Scripture.
- **Practice hospitality:** welcome someone who may feel forgotten.
- **Give thanks:** like the Magi rejoicing at the star, thank God for His guidance along the way.

When we seek Christ with sincere hearts, He reveals Himself, not always in grandeur, but in the gentle light that leads us home.

## Closing Prayer

> Jesus, Mary, and Joseph,
> you welcomed the wise men into your humble
>     abode.
> Teach us to recognize Christ in our midst,
> to offer Him the best of our lives,
> and to welcome others with open hearts.
> Amen.

## Reflection Questions

- What gift can I offer to Christ today: my time, my patience, my talents?
- How can my family live hospitality like Mary and Joseph?
- What "star" of grace (Scripture, prayer, or guidance) is God giving me to draw me closer to Jesus?

## DAY 21

# Simeon's Long-Awaited Joy

*Holy Family, greeted by the pious
Simeon in the temple, pray for us.*

## Opening Scripture

"Now, Lord, you may let your servant go in peace, for my eyes have seen your salvation." *(Luke 2:29–30)*

## The Fulfillment of God's Promise

When Mary and Joseph presented the Child Jesus in the Temple, they met Simeon, a devout elder who had waited his whole life to see the Messiah. Guided by the Holy Spirit, he recognized the infant in Mary's arms as the salvation of Israel and the light for all nations. His joy burst forth in the prayer we still know as the *Nunc Dimittis*: "Now you may let your servant go in peace."

The Catechism teaches: "The Presentation of Jesus in the temple shows him to be the firstborn son who belongs to the Lord. With Simeon and Anna, all the expectation of Israel is fulfilled; Jesus is recognized as the long-awaited Messiah, the 'light of the nations' and the 'glory of Israel'" (CCC 529).

Simeon's story is one of patience rewarded and promises fulfilled. In his frailty, he embodies a faith that never stops watching. St. Ambrose wrote, "He took Him into his arms and blessed God, for whoever holds Christ holds the blessing of God" (Exposition of the Gospel of Luke 2.59). The old man's eyes saw what the world overlooked: not a royal procession, but God's glory hidden in the arms of a young mother.

This encounter reminds us that God's timing is perfect. His promises ripen slowly, like fruit in the sun. Simeon's peace came not from achievement, but from surrender.

## Lessons for Families

- **Mary and Joseph's Obedience:** They brought Jesus to the Temple in humility, showing that every child belongs to God. Families today are invited to entrust their homes and children to Him.
- **Simeon's Watchful Faith:** His patience teaches us to trust God's timing, even when prayers seem unanswered.

- **Generational Wisdom:** The meeting of young parents and an aged man of prayer reveals the beauty of faith passed between generations. The faith of elders strengthens the young, and the vitality of youth renews the old.

Together they form a living bridge: promise meeting fulfillment, patience meeting praise.

## Family Reflection

Whenever I think of Simeon, I picture someone in our own parish, one of those quiet souls who prays in the same pew every week, early and reverent. There's a woman in our church who reminds me of my grandmother. She sits in the front row, hands folded, eyes fixed on Jesus in the tabernacle. I often glance at her and feel both longing and gratitude: longing because my own grandparents passed when our children were small, and gratitude because she reminds me that the faith of the elderly is a gift to the whole Church.

Our children's grandparents live far away, each walking their own path of faith. Distance (both physical and spiritual) can make it hard to share faith across generations. At times, I have wished for that visible example of steadfast devotion within our family, the kind that quietly witnesses to prayer and perseverance. Yet I've come to see that God provides these witnesses in other ways, often through faithful hearts He places in our parish community.

I think of Simeon, who spent his days in the Temple waiting for the Messiah. To those passing by, he likely seemed ordinary, just another old man praying. Yet his hidden faith became the hinge of salvation history: the old covenant meeting the new, hope fulfilled in the arms of Mary and Joseph.

That's what I see when I watch that woman praying in church: a faith that has endured time and trial. She doesn't need to say much; her presence is its own testimony. Watching her reminds me that our family, even without many elders nearby, is still surrounded by a great "cloud of witnesses" (Hebrews 12:1).

Sometimes, the people God places in our parish are meant to remind us that we belong to a larger spiritual family. The Church gives us Simeons and Annas in every generation, those who quietly hold the faith for all of us when our own hands grow weary. Their constancy inspires me to keep showing up, to keep waiting with hope, and to teach my children that faithfulness is not measured in perfection, but in perseverance.

## Living the Temple Encounter Today

- **Honor the wisdom of elders:** Spend time with aging relatives or parish members, listen to their stories, and thank them for their faith.
- **Present your life to God:** Offer your daily routines, work, study, and prayer as gifts of love, just as Mary and Joseph presented Jesus in the Temple.
- **Wait with hope:** When prayers seem unanswered, remember Simeon's patience. God's promises are never forgotten.
- **Pray for each generation:** Ask that the old may bless the young, and the young may renew the old with joy.

The meeting in the Temple reminds us that faith is a family story spanning generations. When we live with patience and gratitude, our homes become small temples where God's promises are fulfilled in love.

## Closing Prayer

> Holy Family,
> who met the pious Simeon in the Temple,
> teach us to trust in God's promises.
> Help us to wait with patience,
> to treasure wisdom across generations,
> and to offer our lives as gifts to the Lord.
> Amen.

## Reflection Questions

- How does Simeon's faithful waiting inspire me in my own seasons of waiting?
- What does it mean for me to entrust my family to God, as Mary and Joseph did?
- How can I learn from the wisdom and prayer of elders in my life?

WEEK 4

# The Path of Holiness in the Home

# DAY 22

# God With Us in Exile

*Holy Family, persecuted and exiled to
a foreign country, pray for us.*

## Opening Scripture

"Rise, take the child and his mother, and flee to Egypt... for Herod is about to search for the child, to destroy him." *(Matthew 2:13)*

## The Light in Exile

Not long after Jesus' birth, Joseph was warned in a dream to take Mary and the Child and flee to Egypt. In the dark of night, they became refugees, leaving behind home and safety. This moment reminds us that from His earliest days, Jesus shared in the hardships of the vulnerable and displaced.

The Catechism teaches: "The flight into Egypt and the massacre of the innocents manifest the opposition of darkness to the light: He came to His own and His own received Him not. Christ's whole life was lived under the sign of persecution" (CCC 530). Even in infancy, the Savior's path was marked by danger and divine protection.

St. John Chrysostom reflected, that God permits these things so that we might learn that His providence does not fail those who are in dangers for His sake (Hom. in Matt. 8). The Holy Family's exile shows that holiness is not tied to comfort or stability, but to trust in God's providence. Even in fear and uncertainty, they remained united in faith and love.

Egypt, the land that once enslaved Israel, became a place of refuge for the Redeemer, a sign that no place, however foreign or unfamiliar, is beyond the reach of God's care.

## Lessons for Families

- **Joseph's Obedience:** At God's command, Joseph acted quickly to protect his family, showing the courage of a father's love. His example reminds families that discernment must lead to action. Faith often takes the form of quiet, decisive choices.
- **Mary's Trust:** Though vulnerable in a foreign land, Mary's faith never wavered. She teaches us to lean on God even when the path ahead is unclear.

- **Jesus' Solidarity:** By entering into exile, Jesus identified with all who suffer rejection and displacement. He remains close to every refugee and every struggling family.

The Holy Family's flight is not just history; it is our story. Each of us, in some way, knows what it feels like to be far from home, to live in uncertainty, or to carry hidden fears. Yet the presence of Christ turns every exile into a place of grace.

## Family Reflection

There have been times in our family's life when we've felt displaced, not physically, but spiritually or emotionally. Seasons when plans shifted suddenly, doors closed, or life became uncertain. In those moments, I've often thought of the Holy Family on their journey to Egypt: the fear in the darkness, the exhaustion of travel, the ache of leaving home, and yet the steady conviction that God was guiding their steps.

My own "Egypts" have not always been on a map but within the heart: times of transition, a move to a new parish, a job that ended abruptly, or friendships that faded without explanation. In such seasons, exile becomes a classroom of trust. Like Joseph, we learn to act in faith; like Mary, to hope without understanding; and like the Child Jesus, to rest in the Father's care even amid the unknown.

Recently, I saw a photograph that I cannot forget: a family walking down a cracked road, carrying small suitcases, their entire lives in their hands. Their faces showed fear and grief, but also resilience and something deeper still: trust. It struck me that this is what faith looks like in motion. The Holy Family once walked that same road, carrying the hope of the world in their arms. God was with them at every step.

That image reminds me that even when the world seems broken, God's providence is unbroken. Faith endures, sometimes quietly, sometimes painfully, but always forward. Our family prays for those displaced by war, persecution, or poverty, for mothers and fathers who carry their children and the little they own, walking toward safety and hope. Their courage mirrors that of Joseph and Mary, who fled into the night to protect the life entrusted to them.

We also pray for the grace to welcome the displaced and the lonely in our own lives, to make room for those who feel like strangers, because that is what the Holy Family once was. Exile, whether physical or spiritual, is never the end of the story. God leads His people home, through long roads and foreign lands, until love itself becomes the place where we rest.

## Living the Exile Today

Families face many kinds of exile: sudden moves, financial strain, illness, or seasons of isolation. The Holy Family teaches that even then, home can become a sanctuary of faith and love.

**Ways to live this lesson:**

- **Pray for families in exile:** Remember refugees, migrants, and those displaced by hardship. If possible, support them with concrete acts of charity and welcome.
- **Pray together in crisis:** When life feels uncertain, pause to say, "Holy Family, stay with us in this exile."
- **Build resilience at home:** Create small rituals of love (time together, evening prayer, words of encouragement) that keep faith alive in hard times.

The God who guided the Holy Family into Egypt still guides us through our uncertainties. He is Emmanuel, God with us, even on unfamiliar roads.

## Closing Prayer

> Holy Family,
> who fled into exile to protect the Child,
> be with all families who face rejection,
> > hardship, or displacement.
> Help us to trust God's providence,
> to protect one another with courage,
> and to create homes of faith and love even in
> > times of trial.
> Amen.

## Reflection Questions

- What "exiles" has my family faced: times of fear, loss, or change?
- How can I imitate Joseph's courage or Mary's trust in those moments?
- How can our family show compassion to those who are displaced or in need today?

## DAY 23

---

# The Hidden Years

*Holy Family, hidden and unknown
in Nazareth, pray for us.*

## Opening Scripture

"And the child grew and became strong; he was filled with wisdom, and the favor of God was upon him." *(Luke 2:40)*

## The School of Nazareth

After returning from Egypt, Mary and Joseph raised Jesus quietly in Nazareth. For nearly thirty years (far longer than His public ministry), the Son of God lived in obscurity, working, praying, and growing within an ordinary family. This "hidden life" is a mystery. God chose to spend most of His time on earth not preaching or healing, but sanctifying the walls of a humble home.

The Catechism calls Nazareth "the school where we begin to understand the life of Jesus... the school of the Gospel" (CCC 533). There, divine love took on the cadence of family life: labor, meals, laughter, fatigue, and prayer. Nazareth teaches that holiness often takes root in unseen corners, in chores done with patience, in shared meals, in quiet fidelity.

St. Francis de Sales reflected that the hidden life of the Holy Family reveals the devotion of the simple, a love constant, gentle, and content to serve without recognition (*Introduction to the Devout Life*, III.1). The world knew nothing of their holiness, yet heaven rejoiced in it. To live the mystery of Nazareth is to find peace in being unseen, to love, to serve, and to trust that God sees what others overlook. In the silence of that hidden home, the greatest love story on earth was already unfolding.

## Lessons from the Hidden Life

- **Mary's Contemplation:** She "treasured all these things in her heart" (Luke 2:51), reminding us to seek God's presence in ordinary moments.
- **Joseph's Steadfast Care:** His work as carpenter and protector shows that labor and responsibility, offered with love, are sacred.

- **Jesus' Growth:** By submitting to His parents, Jesus made obedience and humility the foundation of His mission.

Nazareth is where heaven learned the sound of sweeping floors and hammering nails. It shows that the path to sanctity is paved not with spectacle but with steady love.

## Family Reflection

Our own home life often mirrors Nazareth in quiet ways. One evening, after a long day, we gathered for bedtime prayers. The kids were restless, and I felt distracted. Halfway through, one of them prayed, "Thank you, Jesus, for today, even if it was hard." That simple line stopped me. In that moment, I saw Nazareth: holiness born from faithfulness in small things.

Gratitude often comes easiest to children, who notice grace even in imperfection. Their prayer reminded me that holiness doesn't wait for perfect days; it grows out of ordinary ones. God is as present in our exhaustion as in our joy. Moments like these reveal that holiness is rarely loud or extraordinary. It is love, repeated faithfully, that makes a home sacred.

## Living Nazareth at Home

- **See daily work as holy:** Washing dishes, commuting, attending sports practice, or doing homework can all be offered to God.

- **Practice silence:** Set aside moments of quiet reflection as a family, learning from Nazareth's hiddenness.
- **Welcome simplicity:** Avoid chasing recognition or comparison; holiness grows in humility.
- **End each day with gratitude:** Thank God aloud for one small grace or joy.

When we love faithfully in small things, every home becomes a Nazareth, and the quiet of ordinary life becomes the dwelling place of God.

## Closing Prayer

Holy Family of Nazareth,
hidden and unknown to the world,
teach us to find holiness in daily life.
Help us to treasure quiet moments, to love
    faithfully in small tasks,
and to build homes where God dwells.
Amen.

## Reflection Questions

- What ordinary parts of my day can I offer to God as acts of love?
- How does the hidden life of Nazareth inspire me to live with greater humility?
- What simple family practices can help my home reflect the peace of Nazareth?

# DAY 24

# Obedience Born of Love

*Holy Family, faithful and obedient
to divine laws, pray for us.*

## Opening Scripture

"And he went down with them and came to Nazareth, and was obedient to them." *(Luke 2:51)*

## The Daily Yes

The Holy Family's obedience was rooted in love, not legalism. They were faithful Jews who honored God's law with sincerity of heart. Mary and Joseph observed every commandment not as duty but as devotion: "At the end of eight days, when he was circumcised, he was called Jesus" (Luke 2:21); "When the time came for their purification... they brought him up to Jerusalem to present him to the Lord" (Luke 2:22–23); "His parents went to Jerusalem every year at the feast of the Passover" (Luke 2:41); "He went to the synagogue, as was his custom, on the sabbath day" (Luke 4:16).

Even Jesus, though the Son of God, lived His life as a faithful Jew. He declared, "Think not that I have come to abolish the law and the prophets; I have come not to abolish them but to fulfil them" (Matthew 5:17). In Him, divine love brought the law to perfection. Scripture teaches that "the letter kills, but the Spirit gives life" (2 Corinthians 3:6). The Holy Family lived not by the letter alone but by the Spirit, the Spirit of love. Their obedience flowed from listening hearts. "If you love me, you will keep my commandments" (John 14:15); in Nazareth love became a way of life.

The Catechism calls obedience "the listening of faith" (CCC 144). Mary listened and said yes; Joseph listened in dreams and acted without hesitation; Jesus listened as He grew "in wisdom and in stature, and in favor with God and man" (Luke 2:52). Their obedience was not fearful or mechanical; it was alive, creative, and free. St. Francis de Sales referred to this as the union of our will with God's will, and St. John of the Cross reminds us that "at the evening of life, we shall be judged on love alone."

The Holy Family's fidelity teaches that obedience is not servitude but communion, the art of listening with the heart. In a family, this means parents and children learning to hear one another, to yield in love, and to trust that God's will always seeks our good. Obedience is the harmony of love made visible, the daily yes that turns law into life.

## Lessons for Families

- **Mary's Listening Heart:** Her obedience began in attentive silence: "Behold, I am the handmaid of the Lord; let it be to me according to your word" (Luke 1:38). Her yes opened the door of salvation.
- **Joseph's Courageous Obedience:** Joseph's faith was expressed in swift action. When he awoke, he did exactly as God asked. His quiet promptness protected the plan of salvation.
- **Jesus' Filial Obedience:** The Son of God humbled Himself to learn from Mary and Joseph, showing that obedience and holiness grow together.

St. Irenaeus wrote, "The knot of Eve's disobedience was loosed by the obedience of Mary." In the yes of Mary, and in the steadfast fidelity of Joseph and Jesus, the disobedience of Eden was healed. Obedience restores love's order, a return to harmony with the Creator's heart.

St. Francis de Sales observed, "Obedience is the mother of all virtues," reminding us that love proves itself not in feeling but in surrender. To obey God is to love Him with trust.

## Family Reflection

There was a time when our Sunday mornings were a struggle. The children were small, we were tired, and getting everyone ready for Mass felt like a minor miracle. More than once, someone asked, "Do we have to go?"

Over the years, that question changed. Now our children look forward to Sunday, to friends, to singing, and most of all to receiving Jesus. The shift didn't happen overnight; it grew slowly, through grace and conversation.

We often remind them that the command to keep holy the Lord's Day is not a burden but a gift. The Church teaches that attending Mass on Sundays and holy days is part of God's commandment of love (CCC 2181). We go because we love Jesus, and because Jesus loved us first.

I once told them, "Think of your favorite person in the world, someone you can't wait to be with. That's what Sunday should feel like. We get to be with Jesus, not just in spirit, but really. We receive His Body and Blood; He becomes part of us so we can love like Him."

When I see their joy now, I realize that obedience to divine law is not about checking boxes; it's about showing up for love. Mary and Joseph faithfully observed the law not because they had to, but because they wanted to. Their hearts were tuned to God's will.

Our family's journey from resistance to joy reminds me that love perfects the law. What begins as obligation can, by grace, become delight. When we choose to meet God out of love, obedience becomes communion.

## Living the Spirit of Obedience Today

- **Listen before acting:** Teach that obedience begins in listening, both to God and to one another.

- **Pray as a family:** Prayer aligns hearts to God's will and makes obedience a shared act of love.
- **Find joy in duty:** Do ordinary things with extraordinary love.
- **Embrace freedom in surrender:** Obedience frees the heart from self-will and opens it to peace.

The Holy Family's quiet fidelity shows that obedience is not dramatic; it is daily. Every act of trust, every moment we choose God's will over our own, builds the peace of Nazareth in our homes. In that peace, love learns to listen.

## Closing Prayer

> Holy Family,
> faithful and obedient to divine law,
> teach us to listen with open hearts,
> to trust God's will with courage,
> and to live obedience as love.
> May our homes echo the peace of Nazareth,
> where God's will was done with joy.
> Amen.

## Reflection Questions

- How does the Holy Family's example help me understand obedience as love rather than obligation?

- Where is God inviting me to listen more deeply before acting?
- How can I teach or model loving obedience within my family?

## DAY 25

# Perfect in Love

*Holy Family, perfect model of the Christian family, pray for us.*

## Opening Scripture

"And above all these put on love, which binds everything together in perfect harmony." *(Colossians 3:14)*

## The Model of Perfect Love

When we call the Holy Family the perfect model of the Christian family, we do not mean they lived without conflict or difficulty. There were no perfect circumstances in Nazareth, only perfect love. Their home was marked not by comfort but by faith, patience, and forgiveness.

Mary and Joseph faced poverty, exile, and uncertainty, yet their trust in God transformed every hardship into funnels of grace. Jesus grew up seeing that holiness is not flawless living but faithful loving. In their daily work and prayers, in their simple meals and quiet evenings, love reigned, the kind of love that "bears all things, believes all things, hopes all things, endures all things" (1 Corinthians 13:7).

The Catechism reminds us: "The Christian family is the first school of Christian life and a 'school for human enrichment.' Here one learns endurance and the joy of work, fraternal love, generous —even repeated—forgiveness, and above all divine worship in prayer and the offering of one's life" (CCC 1657).

## Lessons from Nazareth

- **Jesus' Obedience:** The Son of God humbled Himself to obey His earthly parents. His quiet submission sanctifies ordinary family life and shows that harmony at home begins with mutual respect.
- **Mary's Trust:** Her love did not depend on control. She kept her heart open through uncertainty, teaching that trust in God brings peace even in chaos.
- **Joseph's Steadfast Care:** His love was expressed through labor, provision, and protection. He reminds every parent that faithful presence speaks louder than many words.
- **Saint's Insight:** St. Thérèse of Lisieux wrote, "Perfection consists in doing His will, in being what He wills

us to be." In Nazareth, the Holy Family teaches that perfection is not the absence of flaws but the fullness of love.

## Family Reflection

One afternoon I left the kitchen for a few minutes and returned to find water everywhere. What began as innocent play at the sink had turned into a small flood. For a moment I froze. Part of me wanted to shout, to let my frustration spill out as freely as the water.

Then I remembered the words of St. Francis de Sales, who urged us to practice "the little virtues": gentleness, humility, patience, and self-control, the quiet habits that make love endure. I took a breath, knelt beside my child, and gently rubbed her back. "It's okay," I said, "Let's clean this up together." It took everything in me to keep calm, but grace met me there.

As we mopped and laughed through the puddles, I realized that perfection, as Jesus teaches ("You, therefore, must be perfect, as your heavenly Father is perfect," Matthew 5:48), does not mean living without messes. It means letting love guide our response to them. God uses the ordinary accidents of family life to stretch our patience, refine our gentleness, and teach us His steady mercy.

That is the perfection of Nazareth: not flawlessness, but love made faithful in small things. Each time we choose gentleness over anger, humility over pride, or patience over panic, we learn to love as the Holy Family loved, quietly, tenderly, perfectly in spirit if not in circumstance. In such moments, our homes become small Nazareths where divine love dwells unseen yet radiant.

## Living the Model at Home

- Pray together daily, even if it is brief or messy; God blesses effort more than polish.
- Offer everyday work (laundry, dishes, commutes) as gifts of love to God and to one another.
- Ask forgiveness quickly; families grow holy not by avoiding mistakes but by reconciling in love.
- Celebrate small joys (meals, milestones, answered prayers) as reminders that God inhabits the ordinary.

When love governs the smallest things, our imperfect homes shine with divine peace, the reflection of Nazareth in the world.

## Closing Prayer

> Holy Family,
> perfect model of the Christian family,
> teach us that perfection lies in love, not in flawlessness.
> Help us to bear one another's burdens with gentleness and grace.
> May our home reflect the peace of Nazareth,
> where Jesus grew in wisdom and love.

Unite our hearts in faith, patience, and joy,
so that we may live as a true domestic church.
Amen.

## Reflection Questions

- How does my family seek to love one another when life feels imperfect or messy?
- What small acts of patience or forgiveness can help us grow in holiness?
- How can I remember that perfection in family life means perfect charity, not perfect order?

## DAY 26

# Peace That the World Cannot Give

*Holy Family, center of peace and concord, pray for us.*

## Opening Scripture

"Blessed are the peacemakers, for they shall be called sons of God." *(Matthew 5:9)*

## The Gift of Peace

The peace of the Holy Family was not the fragile calm that depends on comfort or control. It was the lasting peace that Christ promised: "Peace I leave with you; my peace I give to you; not as the world gives do I give to you" (John 14:27).

Their peace did not come from perfect circumstances but from perfect trust. Mary and Joseph faced fear, poverty, and exile, yet they remained anchored in God. Jesus, the Prince of Peace, was their constant center.

The Catechism teaches that "earthly peace is the image and fruit of the peace of Christ, the messianic 'Prince of Peace'" (CCC 2305). True peace is both gift and mission: a gift received from the Holy Spirit and a mission to share that peace through mercy and forgiveness. St. Augustine wrote, "Peace is the tranquility of order." It flows from a heart rightly ordered toward God.

St. John Chrysostom taught that a household at peace brings peace also to the Church (Homily on Ephesians 20). The Holy Family shows that peace begins not in nations or policies but in hearts, marriages, and homes surrendered to God's love.

## Lessons from Nazareth

- **Jesus' Presence:** Jesus, the Prince of Peace, sanctified His home simply by being present within it. His quiet nearness teaches that peace begins when we make space for Him in our hearts.
- **Mary's Interior Stillness:** Mary carried the peace of God within her soul. Her silence was not emptiness but adoration, a stillness that welcomed the Word.
- **Joseph's Steady Faith:** Joseph's calm strength arose from trust. Even in dreams he listened to God and acted with serene confidence. His obedience was grounded not in fear but in faith.

The peace of the Holy Family was not passive. It was active, strong, and steadfast, the fruit of love that listens, forgives, and endures.

## Family Reflection

Sometimes, no matter how hard we try, peace feels out of reach. The house is loud, tempers flare, and silence becomes the "silent treatment" instead of serenity. There are nights when the day's frustrations linger, and everyone feels worn thin.

When that happens, we've learned to pray together anyway. We gather (sometimes awkwardly, sometimes in weary silence) and say an Our Father or a Hail Mary. Prayer does not always bring instant calm. Peace cannot be forced; it is a gift of the Holy Spirit (Galatians 5:22). It is grace, given when we offer God our chaos and let His presence settle where our strength ends.

The Catechism reminds us that peace is "the work of justice and the effect of charity" (CCC 2304). Peace grows where love is practiced. It is both God's gift and the fruit of cooperating with His grace. We do what we can (pray, forgive, pause), and God does what we cannot. He restores order to the heart.

That's why we make a deliberate effort to pray together, especially when we least feel like it. Somehow, Jesus meets us in those small acts of faithfulness. His grace comes quietly, not as a rush of emotion but as the steady strength to love again. The peace that follows is not something we create; it is Someone we receive.

## Living Peace at Home

The Holy Family lived a peace rooted in silence and simplicity. It was not the silence of avoidance but the stillness born of knowing God is near.

The Carmelite tradition calls interior silence the dwelling place of God. St. Elizabeth of the Trinity wrote of remaining within our soul as in "a little heaven where the God of peace dwells." Carmelites live in silence not to escape the world but to anchor it in prayer. Their hidden fidelity reminds us that peace begins within before it can flourish without.

Families can share this same spirit amid daily noise. Silence does not mean absence of sound but the presence of stillness, the willingness to pause, to listen, to pray before reacting. Peace grows through gentleness, forgiveness, and humility, through small daily conversions of love.

As St. Augustine said, "peace is the tranquility of order." Peace at home is not achieved by control but by conversion. It grows when we surrender the need to win an argument, when we offer a soft word instead of a sharp one, when we invite Christ into our tension rather than trying to solve it alone.

**Ways to cultivate peace at home:**

- **Pause before reacting:** Whisper a prayer to the Holy Spirit for patience and peace.
- **Pray together daily:** Even short, distracted prayers invite grace into the moment.
- **Embrace holy silence:** Set aside brief times without noise to rest together in God's presence.

- **Forgive quickly:** Peace returns where mercy is given freely.
- **Offer frustration as prayer:** Say, "Lord, this is hard, but I give it to You."

Peace is not something we master; it is Someone we welcome. When Christ reigns at the center of family life, His peace fills every corner of the home, even when life remains imperfect. The quiet of Nazareth still echoes wherever hearts choose to love.

## Closing Prayer

> Holy Family,
> center of peace and concord in the home,
> teach us to welcome the peace of Christ,
> the gift of the Holy Spirit, into our hearts and homes.
> Help us to pause before we speak,
> to forgive when it is hard,
> and to rest in silence when words fail.
> May our homes become small sanctuaries
> where the Prince of Peace finds rest.
> Amen.

## Reflection Questions

- How does my family invite the peace of Christ into our home when tension arises?

- What small habit could help me practice inner stillness each day?
- How can I welcome the Holy Spirit's gift of peace rather than trying to control it myself?

## DAY 27

# Guardian, Provider, Protector

*Holy Family, whose protector is a model
of paternal care, pray for us.*

## Opening Scripture

"When Joseph awoke from sleep, he did as the angel of the Lord commanded him; he took his wife, but knew her not until she had borne a son; and he called his name Jesus." *(Matthew 1:24–25)*

## The Courage of a Father's Heart

Joseph's silent strength anchors the Holy Family. Though Scripture records not a single word from him, his life speaks eloquently of obedience and love. When the angel appeared in a dream, Joseph rose without hesitation and did what God asked. Through his quiet actions (taking Mary as his wife, protecting the Child, fleeing into Egypt), he became the living image of a father's trust.

The Catechism teaches: "Jesus' obedience to his mother and legal father fulfills the fourth commandment perfectly and was the temporal image of his filial obedience to his Father in heaven" (CCC 532). Joseph's fatherhood was not biological but vocational. He embodied the Father's own care through service and sacrifice.

St. John Paul II wrote that Joseph "made his life a service, a sacrifice to the mystery of the Incarnation and to the redemptive mission connected with it" (Redemptoris Custos, §8). Pope Francis calls this Joseph's "creative courage" (Patris Corde, §5), the kind of love that protects without controlling, leads without dominating, and trusts without seeing the whole plan.

Joseph's care mirrors the love of God the Father: protective, steadfast, and tender. Fatherhood, in him, becomes a vocation of discipleship, guarding what is holy, guiding with humility, and trusting that God will provide.

Tradition holds that Joseph was no longer alive when Jesus began His public ministry. Though the Gospels are silent about his death, the Church has long believed he "fell asleep in the Lord" before the Passion. Even here, Joseph teaches that a father's influence endures beyond his presence.

And for families where a father is absent (through distance, loss, or circumstance), Joseph stands near. He is patron and protector for all, a reminder that God's fatherly love is never withdrawn.

# Day 27: Guardian, Provider, Protector

## Family Reflection

In our home, I often see reflections of St. Joseph in my husband. He leads not by command but by example. He is the first to rise for daily Mass, the one who gently reminds us to pray the Rosary, to go to Confession, to keep Sunday holy. His quiet leadership steadies our family; he carries our worries to prayer before he ever speaks of them aloud.

There have been times when life felt uncertain: financial strain, housing questions, decisions that weighed heavily. In those seasons, his steady words have always been the same: "Persevere. Never give up. Pray the Rosary." Those words have become our family's lifeline. They echo Joseph's quiet faith, the conviction that obedience and trust will see us through what we cannot understand.

When we have prayed the Rosary together in times of worry, I have felt what I imagine Mary must have felt beside Joseph: the calm assurance that God provides when we surrender. Watching my husband's faith has taught me that paternal care is more than protection or provision; it is spiritual leadership rooted in hope. His constancy reminds me that love's greatest power lies in perseverance. Like St. Joseph, he guards our family not only with his hands but with his prayers.

For those who no longer have a father present, Joseph's witness brings comfort. He remains the faithful guardian of every family that turns to him, especially those in need of courage, protection, and peace.

## Living Joseph's Example

St. Joseph shows that fatherhood (and every form of Christian leadership) is a call to service. His love was practical and prayerful, a quiet strength that provided safety and nurtured faith.

Every family can live Joseph's virtues in its own way:

- **Lead through prayer:** Even a single "Our Father" prayed together anchors the day.
- **Work with love:** Offer daily tasks of labor for God's glory.
- **Protect the vulnerable:** Defend the dignity of every person entrusted to your care.
- **Trust in Providence:** When answers seem distant, echo Joseph's silent faith: "God will provide."
- **Go to Mary:** As Joseph did, entrust every need to her maternal intercession.

Joseph teaches us that the strength of a father (or of any believer) lies in quiet fidelity. His obedience was his language of love, and through it he reflected the Father's heart. When families walk in this spirit of trust, the peace of Nazareth abides in their homes.

## Closing Prayer

St. Joseph,
guardian of the Redeemer and protector of the Holy Family,
teach us to trust as you trusted,

to labor as you labored,
and to love as you loved.
Bless all fathers and those who act with a
   father's heart.
Be a protector to families who struggle,
and guide us all to persevere in faith and peace.
Amen.

## Reflection Questions

- How does St. Joseph's silent example invite me to lead through faith rather than words?
- What can I do to honor or imitate the fathers and protectors in my life?
- How can my family turn to St. Joseph when we face uncertainty or fear?

# DAY 28

# The Steadfast Heart of Mary

*Holy Family, whose mother is a model of maternal diligence, pray for us.*

## Opening Scripture

"Behold, I am the handmaid of the Lord; let it be to me according to your word." *(Luke 1:38)*

## The Heart that Perseveres

When we speak of Mary's diligence, we do not mean endless activity or tireless efficiency. Her diligence was love made visible, a harmony of action and contemplation. Every task she performed, from drawing water to tending her child, flowed from her "yes" to God.

Mary's diligence was the visible expression of her interior faith. She teaches that true diligence is not restless doing but faithful presence, performing small acts with great love. The Church calls her "the handmaid of the Lord" (Luke 1:38) because her service sprang from humility, not ambition.

The Second Vatican Council teaches that Mary "faithfully persevered in her union with her Son unto the cross" (Lumen Gentium, §58). Her perseverance was her diligence, a steady fidelity to God's plan, whether in the simplicity of Nazareth or the sorrow of Calvary.

St. Francis de Sales taught that "great occasions for serving God seldom present themselves, but little ones are frequent." Mary embraced those little ones completely, sanctifying ordinary home life and teaching us that holiness grows through constancy, patience, and quiet love.

## Lessons from Nazareth

- **Mary's Faithful Service:** Her days were filled with the hidden work of family life, yet each task became a prayer offered to God.
- **Mary's Persevering Love:** She did not turn away from difficulty but met it with faith and peace, knowing that every moment held meaning within God's design.
- **Mary's Joy in the Ordinary:** She shows us that diligence is not drudgery but joy: the grace of cooperating with God's will in daily life.

Mary's diligence was grace in motion: humble, fruitful, and steadfast. Through her, we learn that true strength is quiet and that sanctity is born in the fidelity of love.

## Family Reflection

Although I was raised Catholic, I didn't always have a close relationship with Mary. As a child, I knew her name but not her presence. It wasn't until young adulthood (when I returned to my faith) that I began to pray the Rosary. At first, it felt awkward, like reaching out to someone distant. But slowly, the smoothness of the beads and the repetition of her name softened my heart.

Since becoming a mother, I have come to see her differently. It isn't that one must be a parent to feel close to Mary; her maternal love extends to every soul who seeks her. Yet motherhood helped me glimpse her gentleness in a new way. I imagine her folding linens in Nazareth, stirring a pot of food, or tucking Jesus into bed at night. That image makes her love tangible: faithful, steady, attentive.

There's an old story about someone who, feeling lonely one night, sensed the covers being gently pulled up around them, as if a loving mother were tucking them in. I like to think that was Mary. I have felt that same grace in prayer, those quiet moments when the day's worries ease and her presence feels near.

Now, when I kneel to pray the Rosary after a long day, I feel as though she is tucking me in too, gathering the day's loose ends, smoothing the creases, and wrapping it all in peace. Mary teaches that love is not loud or hurried; it is steady care that remembers, tends, and believes. Her diligence sanctifies the ordinary and turns even our weariness into prayer.

## Living Mary's Example

Mary is the "Lady of the Interior Life" because her diligence flowed from recollection, doing every task with her heart turned toward God. Families can live this Marian spirit in simple ways:

- Begin each day with a quiet "Be it done unto me," renewing trust in God's will.
- Offer work and caregiving as prayer, especially the small, unseen labors of love.
- Keep a Marian image or candle in the home as a reminder of her presence and example.
- End the day with a Hail Mary or a decade of the Rosary, placing the day's joys and burdens in her hands.
- Practice gentleness (Mary's hallmark virtue) in speech, tone, and response.

Mary's maternal diligence belongs to everyone who serves with love. Her example reminds us that holiness is found not in doing great things, but in doing ordinary things with great faith. When we invite her into our routines, she helps us transform daily work into quiet worship, and every task becomes a thread in God's tapestry of grace.

# Day 28: The Steadfast Heart of Mary

## Closing Prayer

> Mary,
> model of maternal diligence and faithful
>     service,
> teach us to unite prayer with work and love
>     with labor.
> Help us to see holiness in the smallest tasks
> and to persevere with joy in all that God
>     entrusts to us.
> Mother of the Word Incarnate,
> keep our homes under your care and lead us
>     always to your Son.
> Amen.

## Reflection Questions

- How can I imitate Mary's quiet diligence in my own home or work?
- What ordinary task could I begin to see as an act of love?
- How does Mary's presence help me find peace in daily faithfulness?

FINAL DAYS

## The Hearts of Nazareth

# DAY 29

# The Harmony of Hearts

*Holy Family, whose Divine Child is a model of filial obedience, pray for us.*

## Opening Scripture

"And he went down with them and came to Nazareth, and was obedient to them. And Jesus increased in wisdom and in stature, and in favor with God and man." *(Luke 2:51-52)*

## The Obedience of Jesus

Jesus' obedience in Nazareth is one of the most beautiful and mysterious aspects of the Incarnation. Though He is the eternal

Son of God, He chose to submit Himself to Mary and Joseph, learning from them as a child learns from parents. His obedience was not a concession to weakness but a revelation of divine strength. The God who commands creation became a child who listened.

Obedience, for Christ, was not about rules; it was about relationship. Every act of submission was an act of love, a continual "yes" to the Father's will.

St. Bernard of Clairvaux wrote, "He who was God subjected Himself to human parents, that He might give children an example of humility and offer parents a pattern of authority" (Sermon on the Circumcision, PL 183:131). Bernard's insight reveals the paradox of Nazareth: the Creator of all chose to be taught by His creatures. The humility of Jesus dignifies human obedience; it transforms duty into love and service into worship.

Through this obedience, Christ reversed Adam's disobedience. "By one man's obedience," writes St. Paul, "many were made righteous" (Romans 5:19). Nazareth thus becomes the first chapter in the redemption of the human heart, where love learns to listen.

## Obedience in Love: A Communion of Hearts

The obedience of Jesus at Nazareth foreshadows the obedience of love St. Paul describes: "Be subject to one another out of reverence for Christ" (Ephesians 5:21). True Christian obedience is mutual. It does not suppress freedom but harmonizes hearts through love. In marriage and family life, this means listening, yielding, and discerning together. Husbands and wives live this when they act not from pride but from reverence, each seeking the other's good first.

St. Paul calls husbands to love their wives "as Christ loved the Church and gave Himself up for her" (Ephesians 5:25). This is obedience expressed as self-sacrifice. Wives, in turn, are called to trust and respond to that love, echoing Mary's own "Be it done unto me according to your word" (Luke 1:38).

St. John Paul II described this as reciprocal submission in love. It is a dance of trust and surrender, where obedience becomes dialogue and authority becomes service. The Holy Family lived this perfectly: Joseph protected, Mary trusted, and Jesus obeyed. Each surrendered to God's will through the love they offered one another.

St. John Chrysostom explained this dynamic with tenderness and clarity, teaching that a husband who desires obedience must first take responsibility for his wife as Christ does for the Church. He taught that husbands must love their wives with the same self-giving care that Christ showed for the Church: a love that protects, sacrifices, and serves. When families live this obedience of love, their homes become small sanctuaries of mutual respect and peace. Obedience ceases to be a burden and becomes a response to love.

## Family Reflection

In our home, my husband and I have a small but meaningful pattern that our children notice. Whenever they ask permission for something (staying up later, reading one more chapter, playing outside a little longer), I often say, "What does your dad think?" They go to him, and he replies, "I'm fine with it if Mom is."

It's a small thing, but over time our children have learned something deeper: that Mom and Dad decide together, in unity. Whatever the answer is, they know it comes from one heart, one will. That mutual deference speaks a truth more powerful than words: love listens before it decides.

There are moments when I don't know the right answer. Deferring to my husband gives me space to pause and pray, and I know he does the same. We trust that God will lead us to the same conclusion because the Holy Spirit is at work in our marriage. Unity doesn't mean perfection; it means we seek the answer together.

I often think of the Holy Family in those moments. Mary and Joseph surely faced decisions that required patience and prayer: when to leave for Egypt, how to provide for Jesus, how to raise the Son of God in an ordinary town. Their harmony was not automatic; it was chosen, sustained by grace.

When our children see us listening to one another, they see obedience as love in action. And when we, as parents, look to God together for guidance, we teach them that true authority flows from humility and trust.

## Living Filial Obedience Today

Obedience grows when love listens before it speaks. It is not imposed but inspired. In families, obedience becomes mutual when everyone seeks the will of God together.

**Ways to live this spirit of obedience at home:**

- Begin decisions with prayer; let discernment, not impulse, lead the way.
- Parents: Guide through patience and example more than command.
- Children: Offer small obediences cheerfully, remembering that love often looks like service.
- Spouses: Practice mutual deference, as St. Paul teaches: "Be subject to one another out of reverence for Christ" (Ephesians 5:21).
- All: reflect on Christ's example ("He humbled Himself and became obedient unto death," Philippians 2:8) and ask how His humility might shape your home.

Obedience in love is not about control; it is about communion. When love listens before it speaks, yields before it demands, and forgives before it blames, family life becomes a reflection of divine harmony. In that quiet harmony, Nazareth lives again.

## Closing Prayer

> Jesus, Divine Child,
> obedient to Mary and Joseph,
> teach us to honor one another in love.
> Help parents to guide with patience and
>     wisdom,
> children to respond with respect and joy,
> and families to live in mutual trust and peace.

May our obedience, inspired by Yours, draw us
ever closer to the Father's heart.
Amen.

## Reflection Questions

- How does Jesus' obedience to Mary and Joseph inspire me to practice humility at home?
- What does loving obedience look like in my relationships today?
- How does mutual submission ("being subject to one another out of reverence for Christ," Ephesians 5:21) shape the way I love?

# DAY 30

# True Riches in Nazareth

*Holy Family, poor in material goods, but
rich in divine blessings, pray for us.*

## Opening Scripture

"Blessed are the poor in spirit, for theirs is the kingdom of heaven." *(Matthew 5:3)*

## Where Love Was the Treasure

The Holy Family's life was marked not by luxury but by love. Their poverty was not deprivation but detachment, a freedom to love without clinging to things. St. Paul writes, "Though He was rich, yet for your sake He became poor, so that by His poverty you might become rich" (2 Corinthians 8:9). In Jesus, divine love embraced simplicity so that we might find our riches in God alone.

The Catechism teaches: "Jesus enjoins His disciples to prefer Him to everything and everyone, and bids them 'renounce all that [they have]' for His sake and that of the Gospel" (CCC 2544). St. John Chrysostom reminds us that Christ "does not praise poverty in itself, but the spirit and choice that despises riches" (Homily 15 on Matthew).

In Bethlehem and Nazareth, blessing was measured not in possessions but in presence. Their home lacked comfort yet lacked nothing of heaven. Every meal, prayer, and act of labor became a hymn of gratitude to the God who provides.

## Family Reflection

There was a Christmas early in our marriage when money was very tight. Our first child had just been born, and all we could afford was a book about the birth of Jesus. It was my last few dollars, but I wanted to offer something, a small token of love on the day we celebrated Love Himself coming into the world.

That night, as I wrapped the little book, I thought of Bethlehem. Jesus, the Son of God, entered the world not in splendor but in poverty. The stable where He was born was likely a small cave carved into bedrock, shared with animals for warmth and shelter. The manger, possibly a simple stone trough, cold and unadorned. The swaddling clothes (linen strips used for newborns or the dead) quietly foreshadowed His mission to give His life for the world.

## Day 30: True Riches in Nazareth

Bethlehem means "house of bread," foretelling the coming of the Bread of Life. His first visitors were shepherds, poor, rough-handed men, outsiders to society. Yet they were the first to kneel and adore. Later came the Magi, wealthy travelers who brought their treasures and homage. Each offered what was theirs to give, forming the first procession of hearts turned toward God.

Tradition and archaeology together offer glimpses into what homes in Nazareth may have looked like. Excavations have revealed first-century stone dwellings built into the rocky hillsides, many incorporating natural caves used for storage or shelter. The Holy Family's home was likely one of these: a single room, dimly lit by a lamp, and a small lower area where animals were brought in at night. It was an ordinary village on the margins of Galilee. Yet from this hidden place, the Savior of the world "grew in wisdom and stature, and in favor with God and man" (Luke 2:52).

From such simplicity came salvation. The humility of these spaces draws us back to the interior poverty of spirit that welcomes God. Holiness does not depend on grandeur but on gratitude.

When I placed that little book beneath the tree, I realized its worth lay not in cost but in love, the desire to give from what little we had, trusting God to multiply it. The Holy Family lived that same truth: love sanctifies what is small. Their poverty was not an obstacle but a doorway for divine abundance.

That Christmas taught me that joy does not depend on plenty. The light of Bethlehem shines brightest in simplicity. Whether in a cave, a modest home, or a crowded apartment,

God comes where He is welcomed. Love fills what the world might call empty.

## Living Simplicity Today

Simplicity is not about having less but desiring less. The saints remind us that the poor in spirit are those whose hearts are free for love. The Holy Family's life invites us to practice that freedom in our homes.

- Begin each day with thanksgiving: name one spiritual blessing before any material one.
- Let family meals be simple yet shared, a time for gratitude, not excess.
- Teach children to give first: before saving or spending, offer something to someone in need.
- Keep one sacred space uncluttered, a reminder that, as St. Teresa of Ávila wrote, "God alone suffices."
- Seek beauty in simplicity: a candle, a prayer, or quiet togetherness can be worth more than the richest feast.

St. Francis of Assisi, who called poverty his "Lady," saw in her not misery but freedom: "Holy Poverty," he wrote, "confounds greed and the cares of this world"(Salutation of the Virtues). The Holy Family lived that freedom perfectly, poor in things yet overflowing with grace. When we live simply, our hearts become wide enough for joy to enter and stay.

## Closing Prayer

> Jesus, Mary, and Joseph,
> though poor in material things, you were rich
>   in grace and love.
> Teach us to live simply and gratefully,
> to find joy in one another rather than in
>   possessions,
> and to trust always in the Father's providence.
> May our homes reflect the humble peace of
>   Nazareth, where love was the greatest
>   treasure.
> Amen.

## Reflection Questions

- How does the simplicity of Bethlehem and Nazareth challenge my idea of abundance?
- What small act of generosity or gratitude can I offer this week?
- How can my family welcome Christ through simplicity and trust in providence?

# DAY 31

## Hidden Yet Holy

*Holy Family, as nothing in the eyes of men,
but so great in heaven, pray for us.*

## Opening Scripture

"Can anything good come out of Nazareth?" *(John 1:46)*

## The Holiness of the Hidden Life

In the eyes of the world, the Holy Family appeared unremarkable. Joseph was a carpenter, Mary a young woman of Nazareth, and Jesus a child from an obscure town with no status or influence. Yet heaven saw differently. The Creator of all chose to live among the poor, to grow up in a small, hidden household where faith, love, and obedience were their treasures.

God delights in raising up the humble to accomplish His greatest works. Mary proclaimed this in her Magnificat: "He has put down the mighty from their thrones, and exalted those of low degree" (Luke 1:52). The mystery of Nazareth teaches that greatness is not found in recognition but in faithfulness; not in success but in surrender.

There was nothing impressive about Nazareth. Its homes were rough-hewn and close to the earth, its streets narrow, its days unremarkable. To travelers, it was a place to pass through, not to remember. Yet the simplicity of that village became the setting of the world's greatest mystery. Within its silence, God chose to hide. The Word who made the stars learned the sound of a carpenter's hammer. Heaven began not in splendor, but in the poverty of a forgotten hill town where love was the only wealth.

## Family Reflection

The story of David and Goliath has always captured my heart. David was the youngest and smallest of Jesse's sons, so insignificant that his father did not even call him when the prophet Samuel came to anoint Israel's future king. Yet God saw what others overlooked. Armed only with a sling and five smooth stones, David faced the giant and triumphed, not through power, but through faith. He knew the battle belonged to the Lord.

Scripture reminds us, "When I am weak, then I am strong" (2 Corinthians 12:10). St. Paul discovered that weakness, when surrendered to God, becomes the channel of His grace. All the saints knew this secret. St. Thérèse called it her "little way" of trust and surrender. St. Mother Teresa said, "We are not called to be successful, but faithful."

The Holy Family lived this same humility. In the world's eyes, they were poor and ordinary, yet their littleness became their strength because it made room for God. Their lives were a continual "yes" to divine providence, proof that dependence on God is not weakness but the foundation of holiness.

I think of this truth often when my husband and I face moments of uncertainty. There have been times when we simply did not know what to do: decisions about work, housing, or family matters that left us unsure. After praying at home, one of us usually says, "Let's take it to the Lord."

We go to the chapel and sit before Jesus in the Blessed Sacrament. Sometimes we pray the Rosary; other times we sit in silence, admitting that we have no answers. Yet peace always comes, not because our problems disappear, but because we've placed them in His hands. In that stillness, I often think of John the Baptist's words: "He must increase, but I must decrease" (John 3:30).

Prayer has taught us that humility is not weakness; it is truth. We are not the heroes of our own story; God is. Like David, we bring the few "stones" we have (faith, perseverance, trust), and God provides the victory. Like the Holy Family, we are learning that being small in the world's eyes opens us to something great in heaven.

## Living Hidden Holiness Today

The hidden life is not a wasted life; it is a fruitful one. God often plants holiness in unseen places so that it may grow without pride.

**Ways to live hidden holiness at home:**

- Offer your limitations to God and let Him work through them.
- When decisions are difficult, pray first and discern together as a family in humility.
- Resist comparison; remember that God's plan for your family is unique.
- Practice gratitude for hidden blessings: the small victories, the unnoticed sacrifices, the quiet joys.
- Trust that what feels small on earth is great in heaven.

Holiness often hides in ordinary faithfulness: in the unseen prayers of a parent, the quiet endurance of hardship, or the simple act of love done without praise. Like the Holy Family in Nazareth, our greatness is found not in being noticed, but in belonging wholly to God. When we live this way, heaven's light shines quietly through our smallness.

## Saintly Insight

St. Paul's words ring true for every Christian home: "When I am weak, then I am strong" (2 Corinthians 12:10). The Holy Family lived this paradox daily, drawing strength entirely from grace. The saints all walked this same path of littleness, knowing that humility opens the door to heaven.

## Closing Prayer

> Holy Family of Nazareth,
> hidden and humble on earth yet glorious in heaven,
> teach us to embrace our littleness.
> When we feel unseen or uncertain,
> remind us that You see us and know our hearts.
> Help us to surrender our weaknesses to God,
> that His strength may shine through us.
> May our hidden acts of love, offered with humility and faith,
> echo Your quiet greatness in heaven.
> Amen.

## Reflection Questions

- What "Goliaths" in my life require me to trust God's strength rather than my own?
- How can I practice humility and dependence on God in my daily decisions?
- In what ways does the Holy Family's hidden life inspire me to find holiness in simplicity?

## DAY 32

# Hope Through the Valleys

*Holy Family, our support in life and
our hope in death, pray for us.*

## Opening Scripture

"Now, Lord, you may let your servant go in peace, according to your word; for my eyes have seen your salvation." *(Luke 2:29–30)*

## Support for Every Season of Life

The Holy Family walked every path of human life: joy, work, weariness, and loss. Their faith teaches that God is present in every season, in laughter and in tears, in strength and in frailty.

Tradition tells us that St. Joseph died in the presence of Jesus and Mary, which is why he is called the patron of a happy death. His passing, surrounded by love, shows that death united with God is not terror but peace. Mary's steadfast presence at the Cross teaches that no suffering is ever faced alone, and Jesus' Resurrection assures us that death is not the end but the doorway to life eternal.

The Second Vatican Council teaches in *Lumen Gentium*, "By her maternal charity, Mary cares for the brethren of her Son who still journey on earth" (§62). The Holy Family remains close to us, accompanying us from the cradle to the grave, our intercessors in life, our consolation in suffering, and our hope at life's end.

## The Valley of Hope

Suffering touches every life sooner or later. Perhaps you've lost someone you love, or endured a painful separation. Maybe someone close to you is ill, or you feel distant from God. To love deeply is to grieve deeply; love makes the heart vulnerable. When someone you love suffers, you share the burden: sleepless nights, quiet prayers, uncertain tomorrows.

The Church teaches that suffering entered the world through sin: "Suffering and death, the evils that weighed upon humanity, are consequences of original sin" (CCC 400). Yet God did not leave us there. Through His Cross and Resurrection, Christ transformed suffering from a curse into a channel of redemption.

## Day 32: Hope Through the Valleys

Scripture promises, "If we suffer with Him, we shall also be glorified with Him" (Romans 8:17), and again, "He Himself bore our sins in His body on the tree, that we might die to sin and live to righteousness" (1 Peter 2:24). St. John Paul II wrote, "Suffering, more than anything else, makes present in the history of humanity the force of the Redemption" (Salvifici Doloris, §27).

The saints knew this truth well:

- St. Thérèse of Lisieux called suffering "the very best gift He has to give us."
- St. Padre Pio assured, "The Cross is the ladder to Heaven."
- St. Francis de Sales named it "the most powerful means of uniting our hearts to God."

Suffering purifies love. It teaches compassion, patience, and surrender. The Holy Family knew hardship: poverty in Bethlehem, exile in Egypt, the Cross on Calvary. Their peace did not come from avoiding pain but from trusting God within it.

When we unite our crosses to Christ's, they cease to be empty weights and become bridges to heaven. Every sorrow shared with Him becomes a seed of resurrection waiting quietly beneath the soil of faith.

Maybe today your own cross feels heavy: a broken relationship, financial strain, chronic illness, or quiet loneliness known only to God. Remember, you are not alone. The same Christ who wept at Lazarus's tomb weeps with you; the same Mother who stood beneath the Cross stands beside you.

Jesus has already spoken the final word. Through His death and Resurrection, He has conquered death once and for all. Alleluia.

## Lessons for Families

- **Mary and Joseph's Care:** Their love for Jesus reminds us that family is meant to be a refuge of comfort and strength in suffering.
- **Joseph's Patronage:** His peaceful death with Jesus and Mary beside him invites us to entrust our own final moments (and those of our loved ones) to Divine Mercy.
- **Jesus' Victory:** His triumph over death gives every believer hope that love endures beyond the grave and that families will be reunited in Him.

## Living This Devotion Today

- Pray daily: "Holy Family, support us in life and be our hope in death."
- When illness, grief, or fear arise, pause to pray; invite Jesus, Mary and Joseph into that moment.
- Visit or pray for the sick and elderly, reminding them that God is near.
- Keep a crucifix or image of the Holy Family at home as a sign that divine love accompanies every stage of life, from the cradle to the cross.

When we let the Holy Family accompany us, even our trials become sanctified. Their presence transforms fear into faith, and sorrow into peace that the world cannot give.

## Saintly Insight

St. Francis de Sales wrote, "Those who hope in God shall never be confounded." Hope is not blind optimism but the calm assurance that God can bring good even from sorrow. Joseph trusted this hope in silence, Mary lived it at the Cross, and Jesus fulfilled it in His Resurrection.

## Closing Prayer

> Holy Family of Nazareth,
> our support in life and our hope in death,
> stay close to us in every trial.
> Strengthen our faith when we are weak,
> comfort us in suffering,
> and lead us to eternal peace in Christ.
> Teach us to live each day with hope,
> knowing that death is not the end
> but the doorway to life everlasting.
> Amen.

## Reflection Questions

- How has the Holy Family been a source of comfort for me or for someone I love in times of suffering?

- What helps me find peace when I face uncertainty about life or death?
- How can I bring hope to someone who is grieving or afraid today?

# DAY 33

## Under Their Protection

*Holy Family, patron and protector
of our family, pray for us.*

### Opening Scripture

"Rise, take the child and his mother, and flee to Egypt, and remain there until I tell you." *(Matthew 2:13)*

### Patron and Protector

As we complete these thirty-three days of preparation, we stand beneath the mantle of the Holy Family and call upon them as patrons and protectors of our homes. When Joseph rose in the night and led Mary and the Child safely into Egypt, he was not only obeying an angel's command; he was showing every believer what faith looks like when it is tested. Mary followed in peace, trusting that if God called them into the unknown, He would also walk beside them. And Jesus, resting in their care, sanctified the journey itself.

That same protection is offered to us. The Church teaches that every Christian home is a domestic church (CCC 1655), a living Nazareth where faith is nurtured, hope is learned, and love is practiced. To entrust our household to Jesus, Mary, and Joseph is to invite heaven's guardianship into the simplicity of ordinary life. They shield not only our bodies but our souls; they strengthen us to persevere in prayer, to forgive quickly, and to face uncertainty with courage.

Mary, our spiritual mother, watches over us with tender concern, just as she once kept every word about her Son "pondered in her heart." Joseph, silent and steadfast, teaches us to guard what is holy, even when the world does not understand. And Jesus, present in every home that calls upon Him, remains the center and peace of all true family life.

To live under their protection is to live in continual trust, to see every day as a journey with God into the unknown. Nazareth and Egypt both remind us that holiness often hides in motion, and that the safest place on earth is wherever we walk in faith together.

When we ask the Holy Family to be our patrons and protectors, we are not seeking an escape from hardship but the grace to face it as they did: with obedience, trust, and love that endures through every trial.

## Living the Grace of Trust

Every family knows what it means to reach the end of its own strength. There are seasons when worries pile high: a child's uncertainty, a financial strain, a difficult decision, or an ache that prayer seems slow to ease. We talk, plan, and try to fix things, yet peace feels far away. Then one of us finally says, "Let's take it to the chapel."

There, before Jesus in the Blessed Sacrament, words often fall away. Sometimes we pray the Rosary; other times we sit in silence, letting His presence settle our hearts. In that quiet, we remember: we are not in control, but we are cared for. God who watched over Mary and Joseph in their exile also watches over us.

I imagine Joseph standing in the doorway of their humble home in Egypt, listening for danger yet trusting God's promise. I think of Mary, rocking the Child and whispering prayers while the future lay hidden. Their faith was not free of fear; it was stronger than fear. Each night, they placed their lives again in the Father's hands.

Our family tries to do the same. When decisions weigh heavy or the path ahead is uncertain, we kneel together and pray, "Jesus, we trust in You." We ask the Holy Family to help us believe that surrender is not weakness but strength, that when we let go, God can act. Every prayer of trust, every moment of peace reclaimed, becomes a small echo of Nazareth.

The Holy Family teaches us that protection is not the absence of trouble but the presence of grace. To live under their patronage is to walk with confidence through life's unknowns, knowing that heaven shelters every home that opens its door to love.

## Living Under Their Patronage

- Consecrate your family to the Holy Family, inviting their protection each morning.
- Keep an image of Jesus, Mary, and Joseph in a place of honor as a reminder that they dwell with you.
- When fear or uncertainty arises, pray aloud: "Holy Family, patron and protector of our family, pray for us."
- Live their spirit through hospitality, service, and forgiveness, the daily works of Nazareth.

To live under their patronage is to rest daily in divine peace, the quiet assurance that the same love that guarded Bethlehem and Nazareth now guards your home.

## Prayer before Consecration Day

>Jesus, Mary, and Joseph,
>As we come to the end of our days of preparation,
>We offer you our hearts and our home.
>Be with us as we prepare to consecrate our family to you.
>Guard us from division and harm.
>Strengthen us in faith, hope, and love.
>Teach us to live in unity and peace,

So that our home may reflect the light of
>   Nazareth.
Prepare our hearts to say "yes" from this day
>   forward.
Amen.

## Reflection Questions

- What does it mean for me to entrust my family's future completely to Jesus through the Holy Family?
- How can we keep Jesus, Mary, and Joseph present in our home after today's consecration?
- In what new way can our family live the spirit of Nazareth each day?

## Consecration Day

Today marks the culmination of our thirty-three days of preparation, prayer, detachment, and growing love for God through the example of Jesus, Mary, and Joseph.

Like St. Louis de Montfort taught in his consecration to Jesus through Mary, this day calls for an offering of the heart, a total giving of self in humility, faith, and love.

The Holy Family of Nazareth stands before us as the living model of consecration:

- Mary gave herself entirely to God with her "yes."
- Joseph offered his whole life in obedience and trust.
- Jesus gave Himself to the Father completely, even unto death on the Cross.

To stand before them is to stand before the mirror of divine love made human, a love that prays, works, suffers, and rejoices together. Consecration is not a ceremony of words, but a covenant of love. It is a deliberate placing of our whole life into the hands of Jesus.

To consecrate ourselves to Jesus through the Holy Family is to enter their spirit of surrender, to allow God to dwell in our homes and hearts, and to belong entirely to Him.

Like Mary at the Annunciation, we stand before the mystery of God's will and boldly proclaim our own *fiat* to the Lord. Like Joseph, we choose obedience in faith, trusting that divine light will guide every step taken in darkness. And like Jesus, we offer ourselves entirely to the Father, through the hearts of those who first loved Him on earth.

This consecration sets us apart to be wholly God's under the tender guidance and protection of the Holy Family.

## Suggested Practices for the Day of Consecration

### Fasting and Simplicity

Keep this day simple and prayerful. If health permits or with the approval of one's spiritual director, fast or eat modest meals in the spirit of penance and detachment. Offer your fast for purity of heart, for the sanctification of your family, and for the intention that Jesus, Mary, and Joseph reign in your home.

## Charity or Almsgiving

Perform an act of charity: a donation, a kind word, a hidden service, or a gesture of reconciliation. Offer it as an act of gratitude for God's mercy and a sign of love toward others.

## Prayer and the Rosary

Pray the Holy Rosary as a family, reflecting on the mysteries of Jesus' life through Mary's eyes. Let each decade become an act of thanksgiving for the grace of these past thirty-three days. As you pray each decade, imagine the Holy Family praying beside you. Let each Hail Mary be an act of gratitude and an offering of trust for the days ahead. The Rosary will keep the flame alive kindled by this consecration.

## Reconciliation

Go to confession if possible. The forgiveness of sins and the grace of starting anew open the heart to receive the fullness of God's love. In the same way, families who seek reconciliation mirror the mercy of Nazareth where Jesus, Mary, and Joseph practiced patience and humility daily. Confession renews peace within each person and restores unity within the home.

## Holy Communion

If possible, attend Holy Mass and receive the Eucharist on this day. This is the supreme act of union with Christ, the living renewal of the consecration you are about to make. In Holy Communion, the union we have prepared for over thirty-three days becomes reality. Our hearts meet with Jesus' heart, and love answers Love.

**Votive Offering**

Light a candle or place flowers before an image of the Holy Family as a visible sign of your offering and the flame of your love.

## Preparation of Heart

Before beginning the act of consecration, take a few moments of silence. Reflect on the life of Christ: His humility, His obedience, His mercy.

Think of Mary's surrender at the Annunciation, Joseph's silent faith, and Jesus' hidden life in Nazareth.

Ask for the grace to imitate their virtues and to let God reign fully in every area of your life.

## Act of Consecration to Jesus through the Holy Family

> O Jesus, our Lord and Redeemer,
> I come before You today to consecrate myself
>   and my family entirely to Your Sacred
>   Heart through the Immaculate Heart of
>   Mary and the chaste, steadfast heart of St.
>   Joseph.

I give You my body, my soul, my thoughts, my
    words, and my actions,
everything I am and everything I will ever be.

I renounce sin, selfishness, and all that separates
    me from You.
I surrender the past, the present, and the future
    into Your hands.

O Mary, my Mother and Queen,
teach me your humility, purity, and faith.
Help me to say "yes" each day as you did at the
    Annunciation.

O St. Joseph, my spiritual father,
guide me in patience, courage, and silent trust.
Protect our family from all evil,
and help us to live with the same love that filled
    your home in Nazareth.

O Jesus, Son of the Living God,
reign in my heart and in my home.
May our family reflect the love of the Holy
    Family,
a home of prayer, mercy, and peace.

Lord, from this day forward, we belong entirely
    to You.
May our lives be lived for Your glory,

our suffering joined to Your Cross,
and our joys united to the joy of heaven.

Holy Family of Nazareth,
make our hearts Your dwelling place.
Amen.

## Closing Meditation

Take a few quiet minutes after your consecration to thank God for His grace. You may wish to pray:

"Jesus, Mary, and Joseph, thank You for receiving my consecration. Guard our family in Your peace and help us to live faithfully each day. May we grow in holiness, persevere in love, and one day find our home with You in heaven."

## Reflection for the Newly Consecrated Family

- Live simply, trusting in providence.
- Begin and end each day with prayer as a family.
- Keep a crucifix or image of the Holy Family as a visible reminder of your consecration.
- Renew your consecration annually, if possible on the Feast of the Holy Family.
- Remember that consecration is not an end but a beginning, the start of a lifelong friendship with Jesus through Mary and Joseph.

## Final Prayer

> May the peace of Christ, the love of Mary,
> and the protection of St. Joseph remain with
> > our household, now and forever.
> In the name of the Father, and of the Son, and
> > of the Holy Spirit.
> Amen.

## A Visible Sign of Your Consecration

Now that you have made your consecration to Jesus through the Holy Family, it is fitting to keep a visible reminder of your promise, something that points your heart back to Nazareth each day.

Consider obtaining a holy image, statue, or holy card of the Holy Family and placing it in a special place of prayer in your home. You might set it near a candle or beside your family Bible or Rosary. Let it become the "heart" of your domestic church, a place where your family gathers to pray, give thanks, and entrust your joys and trials to Jesus, Mary, and Joseph.

Each time you pass by this image, renew your consecration in a simple prayer:

> Holy Family of Nazareth,
> guide and guard our family.
> Make our home a reflection of your love,
> and help us to live in faith, hope, and charity
> > each day.

You may also wish to record the date of your consecration and sign your name beneath a written copy of your Act of Consecration. This simple act turns your decision of the heart into a visible promise of love, a sign that the Holy Family will always have a place in your home and in your life.

## Final Exhortation

The journey of these thirty-three days of preparation and the day of consecration has been one of surrender, faith, and love, a slow, steady turning of the heart toward the peace of Nazareth. But today is not an ending; it is a beginning.

Consecration is not a moment of perfection but a lifelong conversion, a daily "yes" renewed again and again, just as Mary said yes to God each morning of her life. You are now invited to live the mystery of the Holy Family in your own way: to work with Joseph's humility, to love with Mary's tenderness, and to live with Jesus' presence at the center of everything.

The Holy Family will walk beside you. When the road feels uncertain, they will protect you. When faith feels dim, they will remind you that God is near. And when joy fills your home, they will rejoice with you.

Keep praying the Rosary. Keep praying for your children and loved ones. Keep loving one another with quiet courage. Every act of love, no matter how small, extends the light of Nazareth into the world.

## Closing Blessing

> May the peace of Jesus Christ dwell richly in your heart.
> May the tenderness of Mary surround you.
> May the strength of Joseph defend you.
> And may your home, from this day forward,
> be a living reflection of the Holy Family of Nazareth.
> In the name of the Father, and of the Son, and of the Holy Spirit.
> Amen.

The 33-Day Consecration to Jesus through the Holy Family now concludes where it began: in love, humility, and trust. From this day forward, you belong wholly to Christ, under the protection and peace of His Holy Family.

# Family Consecration Certificate

## CONSECRATION TO JESUS THROUGH THE HOLY FAMILY

*"As for me and my house, we will serve the Lord." (Joshua 24:15)*

**On this day, with hearts full of love and trust, we consecrate our family entirely to Jesus Christ through the intercession and example of Mary, His Blessed Mother, and Joseph, His Guardian and Protector.**

We offer to God all that we are: our joys and sorrows, our labors and prayers, our home, our possessions, and our future.

May our family become a living reflection of the Holy Family of Nazareth, a dwelling place of faith, hope, and love.

We promise to keep Jesus at the center of our lives, to honor Mary as our Mother, and to follow St. Joseph's example of humble service and quiet strength. May the Holy Family guard us, guide us, and bring us safely into the eternal home of heaven.

**Family Name:** _____

**Date of Consecration:** _____

**Location/Parish:** _____

*Holy Family of Nazareth, make our hearts your home.*

LIVING THE CONSECRATION

## Christ Forge

# Overview

This section is offered as a practical companion to the consecration, a simple way to remember and live it each day.

Christ Forge is the fire that keeps consecration alive.

In Nazareth, holiness was shaped in silence, in the hammer's ring, the sweep of a broom, the tender word shared at day's end.

Here, in our own homes, that same grace continues to glow.

This final part is an invitation to remain within the warmth of that fire: to learn, to live, and to offer love each day until every ordinary moment becomes extraordinary in God's eyes.

Welcome to the Forge, where the heart is made holy.

# Forged in Love

*"Iron sharpens iron, and one man sharpens another." (Proverbs 27:17)*

Your consecration to the Holy Family is not an ending, but a beginning. You have placed your home in the care of Jesus, Mary, and Joseph. Now comes the joyful work of living what you have consecrated. Holiness is not achieved in a single day, but formed slowly, like iron in the fire, through grace, repetition, and love.

This is the heart of Christ Forge. It is the place where faith becomes habit, and habit becomes holiness. Like a blacksmith shaping metal, God shapes our hearts each day in the forge of family life, through patience, forgiveness, work, laughter, and perseverance. Every small act of love, every quiet sacrifice, every moment of trust becomes part of His refining fire.

At Nazareth, the Holy Family lived this hidden holiness. There were no recorded miracles, no public signs, no grand speeches, only love poured out in daily life. The Christ Forge invites us to return to that same simplicity: to be shaped by grace in the ordinary.

This section offers a way to live your consecration through virtue, the steady practice of doing good out of love for God. Each virtue reflects a quality of Jesus, Mary, and Joseph and invites your family to imitate their life together.

You may notice that the word Christ Forge itself forms an acronym, each letter standing for a virtue that, when lived, transforms hearts and homes:

- **C**harity
- **H**umility
- **R**espect
- **I**ntegrity
- **S**trength
- **T**rust
- **F**orgiveness
- **O**bedience
- **R**esponsibility
- **G**ratitude
- **E**mpathy

Each of these virtues shines through the life of the Holy Family and offers us a path to walk after them.

The Christ Forge is not another 33-day journey; it is the daily continuation of what has begun. It is meant to be lived in small, repeatable cycles: learning a virtue, living it, and offering it to God.

As you move forward, do not be discouraged by imperfection. The forge works not through speed, but through steady love. God refines us gently, one day at a time. If you fall, begin again. The Holy Family stands beside you as master craftsmen, ready to help shape your heart in the image of Christ.

We are metal in the Master's hands, shaped upon His anvil and purified in the fire of His love.

# The Way of the Forge

The Holy Family of Nazareth teaches us that holiness is built through repetition, through the quiet rhythm of love lived day by day. In the Christ Forge, we enter that same cadence: we learn, live, and offer each virtue with Jesus, Mary, and Joseph as our guides. This pattern is simple but powerful. When practiced faithfully, it transforms ordinary family life into a school of holiness.

## 1. Learn It

> *"Take my yoke upon you, and learn from me; for I am gentle and lowly in heart." (Matthew 11:29)*

To learn a virtue is to see it through the eyes of Christ. It begins with Scripture, reflection, and conversation, not with perfection, but with understanding.

**Each virtue in the Forge starts by asking:**

- What does this virtue mean?
- How did Jesus, Mary, and Joseph live it?
- What might it look like in my family today?

As you read, pray, or discuss together, ask the Holy Spirit to illuminate the heart of the virtue. You may find that God reveals something new each time: a gentle correction, a moment of clarity, or an invitation to begin again.

Holiness always begins in the heart that listens and learns.

## 2. Live It

> *"Let us not love in word or speech, but in deed and in truth." (1 John 3:18)*

Once we understand a virtue, we must live it, even if only in small ways. The Forge calls families to practice holiness in the ordinary: through a kind word, an act of patience, or a prayer spoken together. This is where the hidden life of Nazareth becomes real. The Holy Family's greatness was not in grand miracles, but in simple faithfulness.

To live a virtue is to bring it from reflection into routine, to make it a habit of love that shapes the atmosphere of the home.

Each week, choose one small action that embodies the virtue you are focusing on:

- A moment of forgiveness instead of irritation.
- Gratitude expressed aloud at dinner.
- A child's humble act of service.
- Parents taking time to listen with empathy.

No effort is wasted in the Forge. God works through every small spark of love.

## 3. Offer It

> *"Present your bodies as a living sacrifice, holy and acceptable to God, which is your spiritual worship." (Romans 12:1)*

Every act of virtue becomes holy when it is offered back to God. The Forge is not a self-help system, but a way of surrender, an invitation to let God sanctify even the smallest gestures of love.

At the end of each day, pause as a family to thank God for His grace and to offer Him your efforts: successes, failures, and everything in between. A simple prayer such as, "Jesus, Mary, and Joseph, we offer You our hearts today. Shape us in love," begins to turn your home into a living forge where God refines your hearts.

This offering keeps the flame of consecration alive. When love is offered, even weakness becomes strength, and the forge burns brighter.

## A Family Rhythm of Holiness

Families may choose to practice this rhythm in different ways:

- **Daily:** focus on one virtue each week and live its rhythm across seven days.
- **Weekly:** gather for a brief "Family Forge Night," reflect on the virtue, share stories, and pray together.
- **Monthly:** dedicate each month to one virtue, deepening your practice over time.

There is no single right pace. What matters is constancy. The forge works through the fire of perseverance, not perfection.

When families learn, live, and offer together, the home becomes a small Nazareth, a place where grace takes flesh in ordinary love.

In the silence of Nazareth, every hammer strike, every prayer, every shared meal became a hymn of praise.

# The Christ Forge Virtues

The virtues are the gentle fires of Nazareth and the qualities that made the home of Jesus, Mary, and Joseph glow with divine love. Each one reflects the beauty of their hearts and offers a pattern for our own families to follow.

These are not ideals far beyond reach, but daily ways of love, ways to shape our words, our work, and our relationships until we begin to resemble the Holy Family themselves.

## C: Charity

"Love one another as I have loved you." (John 15:12)

- Charity is the warmth of the forge. It is love that gives, serves, and forgives without counting the cost. In Naza-

reth, love was spoken through actions, in meals shared, tools passed, and smiles exchanged. Charity transforms homes into havens of peace.
- **Prayer:** "Lord Jesus, teach us to love as You love, with gentleness, generosity, and joy."

## H: Humility

"Learn from me, for I am gentle and humble of heart." (Matthew 11:29)

- Humility opens the door for grace. Mary bowed her heart in every circumstance, Joseph obeyed in silence, and Jesus chose the hidden life of Nazareth. Where humility dwells, peace follows.
- **Prayer:** "Holy Family of Nazareth, help us to serve one another quietly and to rejoice when others are lifted high."

## R: Respect

"Outdo one another in showing honor." (Romans 12:10)

- Respect is love that listens. It sees Christ in the other person, in the tired parent, the restless child, the neighbor in need. At Nazareth, the Holy Family spoke with kindness and looked with compassion. Respect turns daily life into worship.

- **Prayer:** "Jesus, Mary, and Joseph, teach us to honor each person as a child of God and to speak words that heal, not harm."

## I: Integrity

**Scripture: "Blessed are the pure in heart, for they shall see God." (Matthew 5:8)**

- Integrity is being true in all things: faithful in work, honest in speech, steady in love. Joseph's quiet strength, Mary's constancy, and Jesus' obedience reveal the beauty of truth lived simply. Integrity unites heart and action.
- **Prayer:** "Lord, make our hearts pure and our words sincere, that truth may dwell within our home."

## S: Strength

**"The Lord is my strength and my shield." (Psalm 28:7)**

- Strength is courage born of love, not loud or proud, but steady and enduring. The Holy Family faced exile, poverty, and uncertainty, yet their faith never wavered. Their strength was trust in God's promise.
- **Prayer:** "Jesus, Mary, and Joseph, be our strength when we are weary, and our peace when we are afraid."

## T: Trust

**"Trust in the Lord with all your heart."** (Proverbs 3:5)

- Trust is the heartbeat of Nazareth, the confidence that God is working even when we do not see. Mary trusted in the angel's message; Joseph trusted in his dreams; Jesus trusted in His Father's will. Trust transforms worry into worship.
- **Prayer:** "Holy Family, help us to place every fear into God's hands and to rest in His providence."

## F: Forgiveness

**"Forgive as the Lord has forgiven you."** (Colossians 3:13)

- Forgiveness heals what anger divides. At Nazareth, mercy was lived quietly, through patience, understanding, and reconciliation. Where forgiveness reigns, joy returns.
- **Prayer:** "Lord Jesus, soften our hearts to forgive quickly, that peace may dwell within our home."

## O: Obedience

**"Blessed are those who hear the word of God and obey it."** (Luke 11:28)

- Obedience is love that listens and responds. Mary's *fiat*, Joseph's action, and Jesus' surrender show that obedience is not weakness, but freedom in God's will. It is the harmony of hearts that trust God's voice together.
- **Prayer:** "Holy Family, help us to say "yes" to God each day and to follow His will with joy."

## R: Responsibility

**"Each of you should look not only to your own interests, but also to the interests of others." (Philippians 2:4)**

- Responsibility is love made reliable. Joseph worked faithfully, Mary guided tenderly, and Jesus grew in wisdom through obedience. Every act of care (every dish washed, every task completed) becomes service to God.
- **Prayer:** "Lord, teach us to carry our daily duties with love, and to serve one another with cheerful hearts."

## G: Gratitude

**"Give thanks in all circumstances." (1 Thessalonians 5:18)**

- Gratitude turns ordinary life into praise. Mary's Magnificat, Joseph's quiet faith, and Jesus' blessing over bread reveal hearts that never ceased to thank God. A thankful home becomes radiant with peace.

- **Prayer:** "Heavenly Father, open our eyes to Your blessings and fill our hearts with thanksgiving each day."

## E: Empathy

**"Rejoice with those who rejoice; weep with those who weep." (Romans 12:15)**

- Empathy is love that feels with others. The Holy Family shared one another's joys and sorrows, laughing, working, and weeping together. Empathy is the tenderness of God reflected in human hearts.
- **Prayer:** "Jesus, Mary, and Joseph, make our hearts gentle and compassionate, that no one in our family feels alone."

The forge burns hottest when love is lived quietly. In every act of charity, humility, or patience, the fire of Nazareth is rekindled within us.

# How to Practice the Forge at Home

*"Whatever you do, in word or deed, do everything in the name of the Lord Jesus, giving thanks to God the Father through Him." (Colossians 3:17)*

Consecration plants the seed of holiness; daily practice waters it. The Forge is not a new burden but a way of grace woven into ordinary life, one that strengthens the heart and sanctifies the home. You don't need elaborate plans or long prayers. You only need intention, the desire to invite Jesus, Mary, and Joseph into the small details of family life.

## Begin with a Simple Prayer

Each morning or evening, gather your family (even briefly) and pray:

> Jesus, Mary, and Joseph, forge our hearts in love today. Teach us to learn, live, and offer each moment to You.

This simple invocation keeps the flame of consecration alive. It reminds the heart that holiness grows one moment, one choice at a time.

## Choose One Virtue at a Time

Select one of the Christ Forge virtues to focus on for a few days or a full week. Let that virtue quietly guide your family's thoughts and actions. You might:

- Write the virtue's word on a card and place it near your family's prayer space.
- Read its Scripture verse aloud at breakfast or bedtime.
- Invite each person to share one way they noticed that virtue during the day.

Even young children understand these practices: a kind word, a small act of help, a moment of forgiveness.

## Keep the Forge Small and Steady

The Forge is strongest when practiced gently. Ten minutes a day is enough:

- Read the day's virtue or Scripture.
- Reflect together on how you lived it.
- End with gratitude and a short prayer.

If a day is missed, simply begin again. Holiness is not a straight line but a circle of mercy. God does not measure perfection, but faithfulness.

## Create a "Nazareth Moment" Each Week

Once a week, pause as a family for a short time of reflection. Light a candle or gather around your table and share:

- Where did we see God's love this week?
- When did we struggle to live our virtue?
- What can we offer to the Lord with gratitude?

You may choose to close this time with a simple act of love: a hug, a word of forgiveness, or a prayer for another family. These small rituals shape the soul more deeply than grand gestures ever could.

## Let Ordinary Life Become the Forge

Holiness is not separate from laundry, homework, errands, or bills. It is forged within them. Each task done with love becomes an offering. Each trial accepted with patience becomes a spark in God's fire.

The Holy Family lived holiness in the hidden life of Nazareth: Joseph at his bench, Mary in her quiet service, and Jesus growing in wisdom. Your family's daily life is your Nazareth, the place where love takes root.

Every nail Joseph drove, every meal Mary prepared, every word Jesus spoke was sanctified by love.

Let every moment of your day (the noise, the stillness, the laughter, the tears) become part of your offering to God.

## Return to the Forge Often

Whenever the home feels weary or divided, return to the Forge. Choose one virtue and begin again (perhaps Forgiveness or Trust) and let its grace renew you.

The Holy Family will meet you there. They know the fatigue of work, the uncertainty of exile, and the hidden joys of love. They are patient teachers and faithful companions.

"And let us not grow weary in well-doing, for in due season we shall reap, if we do not lose heart." (Galatians 6:9)

Every act of love rekindles the fire of Nazareth. Every small virtue lived becomes an offering that glows in God's sight.

# Prayer of Renewal: Lord, Forge Our Hearts in Love

*"He will sit as a refiner and purifier of silver, and he will purify the sons of Levi and refine them like gold and silver, till they present right offerings to the Lord." (Malachi 3:3)*

Jesus, Mary, and Joseph,
You are the Holy Family, the radiant light of Nazareth, the hearth where divine love burned in silence and joy.
You have shown us that holiness begins not in grand gestures, but in the hidden places, in the patient rhythm of work, in the laughter of children, in the quiet offering of each day.
Forge our hearts in that same love.
Make our home a living Nazareth, a place

where kindness conquers anger, where forgiveness restores peace, where gratitude lifts the weary heart.

Teach us to learn, live, and offer all things for love of You.

When we grow impatient, remind us that grace works slowly, shaping us as fire shapes iron.

When we fall short, draw us back into Your mercy, that we may begin again without fear.

Bless the work of our hands, the words of our mouths, and the silence of our hearts.

Let every act of service, every trial endured, every joy shared become a spark that unites us more deeply to You.

Jesus, forge our hearts in charity.

Mary, mold our hearts in humility.

Joseph, strengthen our hearts in faith.

Together, keep our family within the flame of God's love.

May this consecration bear fruit that endures: peace in our home, gentleness in our speech, and steadfast love that endures all things.

And when our days on earth are done, may

we take our place beside You, Lord, in the eternal home prepared for those who love You.

Holy Family of Nazareth, patron and protector of our family, pray for us now and at the hour of our death.

Amen.

*The fire of Nazareth never dies; it burns wherever love is lived for God.*

# Appendices

ADDENDUM I

# A Pilgrimage of the Heart

*Pilgrimage is not only a journey of the feet but of the heart. Whether through prayer, reading, or travel, may these sacred places help you draw nearer to Jesus, Mary, and Joseph.*

The Holy Family is revered in Catholic devotion as the model of family life. Across the world, major churches, cathedrals, and shrines have been formally dedicated to the Holy Family. Some hold the status of minor basilicas or national shrines conferred by the Vatican or local bishops, while others serve as diocesan cathedrals or pilgrimage centers.

This section surveys prominent Holy Family sanctuaries, emphasizing places recognized by the Catholic Church.

This part is like a mini spiritual travelogue, inviting readers to "visit" these places spiritually even if they cannot go physically.

From Nazareth's humble grotto to distant villages and bustling cities, each sanctuary devoted to Jesus, Mary, and Joseph tells the same story of faith, protection, and love.

To visit these places (even in spirit) is to continue your journey of consecration. Whether you travel with your feet or with your heart, may this pilgrimage draw you deeper into the mystery of Nazareth, where divine love took flesh in the midst of ordinary life.

> *Go forth, then, pilgrim soul. The Holy Family awaits you at every altar, every hearth, every home where love is lived for God.*

## Vatican-Approved Minor Basilicas & National Shrines

### Basílica de la Sagrada Família

*Barcelona, Spain (Minor Basilica)*

- **Status:** Minor Basilica (consecrated and elevated by the Holy See).
- **Brief History:** Begun in 1882 and entrusted to Antoni Gaudí in 1883, the Sagrada Família developed into a unique synthesis of Scripture, liturgy, and Catalan craft. Its Nativity, Passion, and Glory façades narrate salvation history in stone and light. The church was solemnly consecrated and proclaimed a minor basilica by the Holy See.

- **Significance & Devotional Role:** Dedicated explicitly to Jesus, Mary, and Joseph, it is among the world's most visited Catholic churches and a magnet for pilgrim catechesis through beauty. Its towers and symbolic artwork invite families to contemplate the hidden life of Nazareth and the Paschal Mystery. The basilica's global draw makes it a universal shrine of family holiness.
- **Note on Recognition:** Possesses the papal title of basilica minor.

## Cathedral Basilica of the Holy Family

*Nairobi, Kenya (Cathedral & Minor Basilica)*

- **Status:** Metropolitan cathedral of the Archdiocese of Nairobi; elevated as a minor basilica by the Holy See.
- **Brief History:** Constructed in the decades surrounding Kenya's independence, it was consecrated as the mother church of the archdiocese. The basilica title was later granted, recognizing its importance in the life of the Church in East Africa.
- **Significance & Devotional Role:** With vibrant liturgy and immense pastoral outreach, it presents the Holy Family as the heart of Christian life for countless Kenyan households. Stained glass and devotional art emphasize Nazareth's virtues of work, prayer, and charity. It stands as a national point of unity for families and pilgrims.
- **Note on Recognition:** Holds both cathedral rank and the papal title of basilica minor.

### Archcathedral Basilica of the Holy Family

*Częstochowa, Poland (Archcathedral & Minor Basilica)*

- **Status:** Seat of the Metropolitan Archdiocese of Częstochowa; also an archcathedral and minor basilica.
- **Brief History:** Built in the early 20th century in neo-Gothic style, it became the diocesan cathedral when the see was erected and later the archcathedral upon metropolitan elevation. Its dedication honors Jesus, Mary, and Joseph in a nation deeply marked by Marian devotion.
- **Significance & Devotional Role:** As Poland's principal cathedral under this title, it hosts major archdiocesan liturgies and family-focused pilgrimages. The sanctuary presents the Holy Family as model and intercessor for fidelity amid trial. It complements nearby national devotions by rooting them in the daily holiness of home life.
- **Note on Recognition:** Officially listed as a basilica minor while serving as metropolitan cathedral.

### Santuário Basílica Sagrada Família

*Goiânia, Brazil (Minor Basilica & Shrine)*

- **Status:** Parish sanctuary elevated to perpetual adoration shrine and later to basilica minor by the Holy See.
- **Brief History:** Founded in the late 20th century, the church grew into a bustling sanctuary offering daily confessions and Eucharistic adoration. Its elevation to

basilica recognized extraordinary pastoral fruitfulness and stable devotion to Jesus, Mary, and Joseph.
- **Significance & Devotional Role:** Welcoming immense weekly congregations, it blends family catechesis, social outreach, and robust sacramental life. The motto "Jesus, Maria e José" shapes its preaching, ministries, and pilgrimage culture. Open day and night, it invites families to make their homes "little Nazareths."
- **Note on Recognition:** Formally granted the papal title of basilica minor.

## Basilica of the Annunciation

### *Nazareth, Israel (Major Sanctuary & Basilica)*

- **Status:** Latin Catholic basilica in Nazareth, entrusted to the Franciscans; principal Marian–Holy Family sanctuary of the Holy Land.
- **Brief History:** Built over the traditional grotto where the Archangel Gabriel greeted the Virgin Mary, the present basilica was completed in the 20th century over earlier Byzantine and Crusader foundations. The lower basilica preserves the Grotto; the upper basilica gathers national Marian images from around the world.
- **Significance & Devotional Role:** As the place where the Word became flesh, it marks the threshold of the Holy Family's story and the domestic sanctity of Nazareth. Pilgrims venerate the mystery of the Incarnation and ask for grace to imitate Mary's *fiat* and Joseph's

obedience. It is the Holy Land's preeminent locus for meditating on family holiness.
- **Note on Recognition:** Recognized by the Holy See as a minor basilica and principal pilgrimage site of the Latin Church in the Holy Land.

# National Shrines

## Ukrainian Catholic National Shrine of the Holy Family

*Washington, D.C., USA*

- **Status:** National Shrine of the Ukrainian Greek Catholic Church in the United States; under the spiritual jurisdiction of the Ukrainian Catholic Archeparchy of Philadelphia and in full communion with the Holy See.
- **Brief History:** Founded in the latter part of the 20th century, the shrine arose as a central place of worship for Ukrainian Catholics in America. Standing about a half-mile north of the Basilica of the National Shrine of the Immaculate Conception, it serves as a visible bridge between Eastern and Western Catholic spirituality. Its design and founding mission were shaped by a community seeking a national home where their liturgical and cultural identity could flourish in harmony with the wider Church.
- **Significance & Devotional Role:** The shrine unites the beauty of Byzantine worship with devotion to the

Holy Family as a universal model of faith and perseverance. Its iconography depicts Jesus, Mary, and Joseph in traditional Byzantine art, while the celebration of the Divine Liturgy in both Ukrainian and English fosters communion among generations of the faithful. Pilgrims are drawn to this sanctuary to find hope, continuity, and peace amid the trials of exile and cultural transition.
- **Note on Recognition:** Recognized by the United States Conference of Catholic Bishops as the National Shrine of the Ukrainian Catholic Church and placed under the authority of the Holy See through the Dicastery for the Eastern Churches.

# Recognized Pilgrimage Shrines and Churches (Locally Approved)

## Church of St. Joseph

### *Nazareth, Israel (Parish Church)*

- **Status:** Parish church and traditional site of Joseph's home and workshop; recognized locus of pilgrimage in the Latin Patriarchate.
- **Brief History:** Built near the Basilica of the Annunciation over remains associated by tradition with Joseph's house and a first-century workshop. The present structure overlays earlier chapels venerated by pilgrims for centuries.

- **Significance & Devotional Role:** The site invites reflection on Joseph's hidden sanctity and the dignity of work learned by Jesus in Nazareth. Pilgrims pray for fathers, craftsmen, and families striving for steady virtue. Silence and simplicity make it a school of Nazareth's everyday holiness.
- **Note on Recognition:** Maintained under the local ordinary's authority as part of the Holy Land's established pilgrimage circuit.

## Holy Family Shrine

### *Gretna, Nebraska, USA (Diocesan Shrine)*

- **Status:** A Roman Catholic shrine located along Interstate 80 outside of Omaha near the town of Gretna.
- **Brief History:** Raised as a glass and wood chapel on a hill above the plains, the shrine was established to welcome travelers with prayer, confession, and Eucharistic adoration. It quickly became a beloved way-station for families traveling.
- **Significance & Devotional Role:** Transparent walls symbolize the clarity and openness of Christian family life under God's light. Retreats, devotions, and quiet visits foster healing and reconciliation. The shrine's simplicity mirrors Nazareth's hidden life and invites busy families to pause.

- **Note on Recognition:** Formally designated a diocesan shrine by the local ordinary.

## Church of the Holy Family

### Chicago, Illinois, USA (Historic Parish Church)

- **Status:** Historic parish of the Archdiocese of Chicago; recognized as a major Jesuit foundation and preserved as a sacred heritage site.
- **Brief History:** Founded in 1857, it served waves of immigrants and became one of the city's most significant Catholic landmarks, surviving the Great Chicago Fire. Restored and maintained, it continues as a house of prayer and evangelization.
- **Significance & Devotional Role:** Dedicated to Jesus, Mary, and Joseph, the church bears witness to the Holy Family's companionship with newcomers, workers, and the poor. Its ministries, architecture, and memory inspire fidelity amid urban challenges. Pilgrims come to give thanks for family life sustained through hardship.
- **Note on Recognition:** While not a basilica, it is an archdiocesan landmark with sustained ecclesial approval and pastoral mission.

# Conclusion

The Holy Family is venerated across continents through basilicas, cathedrals, and shrines. Some have become worldwide icons and were proclaimed minor basilicas by the Holy See. Others have been designated national shrines by bishops' conferences or elevated by diocesan bishops as important centers of pilgrimage. Even smaller cathedrals serve as mother churches for their dioceses.

These sites collectively witness to the universal Catholic devotion to Jesus, Mary, and Joseph, inspiring families and pilgrims to emulate their virtues.

ADDENDUM II

# Family Devotional Prayers

*"Jesus, Mary, and Joseph, in you we contemplate the splendor of true love; to you we turn with trust." (Pope Francis, Amoris Laetitia)*

The Holy Family of Nazareth is the living model of holiness in ordinary life. Prayer to Jesus, Mary, and Joseph strengthens families, heals divisions, and renews love in the heart of the home.

The following prayers may be used for personal devotion, during family prayer times, or on the feast day selected for your consecration.

## Prayer for Family Unity

Lord Jesus,
You made Your home in Nazareth
with Mary and Joseph in love and peace.
Look kindly upon our family.

Heal what is wounded, strengthen what is
  weak,
and renew what has grown cold.
May our home reflect Your mercy and joy,
and may we always recognize Your presence in
  one another.
Holy Family of Nazareth,
make our home a place of prayer, a school of
  virtue,
and a refuge of faith.
Amen.

## Prayer for Parents

Mary and Joseph, guardians of the Child Jesus,
teach us to love as you loved,
patiently, faithfully, and without fear.
Help us guide our children toward holiness
  and peace.
When our strength falters,
remind us that God's grace fills what we lack.
Holy Family,
watch over every parent called to mirror God's
  creative love.
Let us raise our children not for this world
  alone,
but for the Kingdom of Heaven.
Amen.

# Addendum II: Family Devotional Prayers

## Prayer for Children

Dear Jesus,
You grew in wisdom and grace in Your home at Nazareth.
Help me to obey, to listen, and to love.
Bless my parents and teachers,
and make my heart kind and joyful.
Mary, my mother, pray for me.
Joseph, my protector, guide me.
Jesus, my friend, stay with me always.
Amen.

## Prayer for Peace in the Home

Holy Family of Nazareth,
You knew the struggles of ordinary life: work
and weariness, misunderstanding and loss.
Yet love never failed within Your walls.
Grant us that same peace.
Still our anxious hearts, soften our speech,
and help us forgive one another quickly.
May our home become another Nazareth,
where God is loved,
neighbor is welcomed,
and heaven is glimpsed in daily life.
Amen.

## Prayer Before a Family Meal

Bless us, O Lord,
and these Thy gifts which we are about to
receive from Thy bounty
through Christ our Lord.
Amen.
Jesus, Mary, and Joseph, we thank You for this food,
for the love that gathers us,
and for the joy of family.
May this meal strengthen our bodies,
and may our hearts remain united in Your peace.
Amen.

## Closing Reflection

*In the house of Nazareth, God sanctified family life. Let every Christian home become a living sanctuary of love, where Christ is known, Mary is honored, and Joseph is imitated.*

# Bibliography

## Preparing the Heart: Foundations of Consecration

**Catechism of the Catholic Church**
*Catechism of the Catholic Church.* 2nd ed. Washington, DC: United States Catholic Conference, 2000.

**Magisterial and Papal Sources**
Benedict XVI. *Jesus of Nazareth: The Infancy Narratives.* Translated by Philip J. Whitmore. San Francisco: Ignatius Press, 2012.
Francis. *Amoris Laetitia (On Love in the Family).* Vatican City: Libreria Editrice Vaticana, 2016.
———. *Patris Corde (A Father's Heart).* Vatican City: Libreria Editrice Vaticana, 2020.
John Paul II. *Familiaris Consortio (The Role of the Christian Family in the Modern World).* Vatican City: Libreria Editrice Vaticana, 1981.

———. *Redemptoris Custos (Guardian of the Redeemer)*. Vatican City: Libreria Editrice Vaticana, 1989.

Paul VI. "Homily at Nazareth." January 5, 1964. Vatican.va.

**Theological and Spiritual Works**

Augustine. *De Trinitate*. Translated by Edmund Hill, O.P. Hyde Park, NY: New City Press, 1991.

Louis de Montfort. *True Devotion to Mary*. Rockford, IL: TAN Books, 2010.

# The 33-Days Of Preparation

**Sacred Scripture**

*The Holy Bible: Revised Standard Version – Catholic Edition*. San Francisco: Ignatius Press, 2006.

**Catechism of the Catholic Church**

*Catechism of the Catholic Church*. 2nd ed. Washington, DC: United States Catholic Conference, 2000.

**Magisterial and Papal Sources**

Francis. *Amoris Laetitia (On Love in the Family)*. Vatican City: Libreria Editrice Vaticana, 2016.

John Paul II. *Dives in Misericordia (Rich in Mercy)*. Vatican City: Libreria Editrice Vaticana, 1980.

———. *Letter to Families (Gratissimam Sane)*. Vatican City: Libreria Editrice Vaticana, 1994.

———. *Man and Woman He Created Them: A Theology of the Body*. Translated by Michael Waldstein. Boston: Pauline Books & Media, 2006.

———. *Redemptoris Custos (Guardian of the Redeemer)*. Vatican City: Libreria Editrice Vaticana, 1989.

———. *Salvifici Doloris (On the Christian Meaning of Human Suffering)*. Vatican City: Libreria Editrice Vaticana, 1984.

Leo XIII. *Neminem Fugit (On Devotion to St. Joseph)*. Vatican City: Libreria Editrice Vaticana, 1892.

Pius IX. *Quemadmodum Deus (On the Patronage of St. Joseph)*. Vatican City: Libreria Editrice Vaticana, 1870.

Second Vatican Council. *Lumen Gentium (Dogmatic Constitution on the Church)*. Vatican City: Libreria Editrice Vaticana, 1964.

## Spiritual and Devotional Works

Ambrose. *Exposition of the Gospel of Luke*. Translated by Theodosia Tomkinson. Etna, CA: Center for Traditional Orthodox Studies, 2003.

Bernard of Clairvaux. *Sermons on the Song of Songs*. Kalamazoo, MI: Cistercian Publications, 1971.

Bonaventure. *Breviloquium*. Translated and edited by Dominic V. Monti, O.F.M. Works of St. Bonaventure, Vol. 9. St. Bonaventure, NY: Franciscan Institute Publications, 2005.

Chrysostom, John. *Homilies on Ephesians*. Translated by W. J. Copeland, edited by Philip Schaff, vol. 13, Nicene and Post-Nicene Fathers, First Series, Hendrickson Publishers, reprint.

———. *Homilies on the Gospel of Matthew*. Translated by George Preston, Oxford: John Henry Parker, 1843.

Elizabeth of the Trinity. *Complete Works*. Vol. 1. Washington, DC: ICS Publications, 1984.

Francis de Sales. *Introduction to the Devout Life*. New York: Image Books, 1989.

Francis of Assisi. *The Writings of St. Francis of Assisi*. Quaracchi Edition. Translated by Paschal Robinson. Philadelphia: The Dolphin Press, 1906.

Gregory the Great. *Homilies on the Gospels*. Translated by Dom David Hurst, O.S.B. Kalamazoo, MI: Cistercian Publications, 1990.

Gregory Nazianzen. *Orations*. In *Nicene and Post-Nicene Fathers*, 2nd series, Vol. 7. Edited by Philip Schaff and Henry Wace. Peabody, MA: Hendrickson, 1994.

Irenaeus. *Against Heresies*. Translated by Dominic J. Unger. New York: Paulist Press, 1992.

John of the Cross. *The Collected Works of St. John of the Cross: The Reader's Digital Edition*. Translated by David Lewis. Charlotte, NC: TAN Books, 2020.

Leo the Great. *Sermons*. Translated by Jane Paterson. Washington, DC: Catholic University of America Press, 1957.

Pio of Pietrelcina. *Letters and Writings of Padre Pio*. San Giovanni Rotondo: Edizioni Padre Pio da Pietrelcina, 2002.

Teresa of Calcutta. *A Simple Path*. New York: Ballantine Books, 1995.

Thérèse of Lisieux. *Story of a Soul*. Washington, DC: ICS Publications, 1996.

## Liturgical and Pastoral Sources

Congregation for Divine Worship and the Discipline of the Sacraments. *Directory on Popular Piety and the Liturgy: Principles and Guidelines*. Vatican City: Congregation for Divine Worship and the Discipline of the Sacraments, 2002.

*Manual of Indulgences*. 4th ed. Washington, DC: USCCB Publishing, 2017.

*The Roman Missal*. Washington, DC: USCCB Publishing, 2011.

# Living the Consecration: Christ Forge

## Scriptural Foundations

*The Holy Bible: Revised Standard Version—Catholic Edition*. San Francisco: Ignatius Press, 2006.

## Magisterial and Papal Sources

Francis. *Amoris Laetitia (On Love in the Family)*. Vatican City: Libreria Editrice Vaticana, 2016.

———. *Gaudete et Exsultate (On the Call to Holiness in Today's World)*. Vatican City: Libreria Editrice Vaticana, 2018.

John Paul II. *Novo Millennio Ineunte (At the Beginning of the New Millennium)*. Vatican City: Libreria Editrice Vaticana, 2001.

Leo XIII. *Neminem Fugit (On Devotion to St. Joseph)*. Vatican City: Libreria Editrice Vaticana, 1892.

Paul VI. "Homily at Nazareth." January 5, 1964. Vatican.va.
Second Vatican Council. *Lumen Gentium (Dogmatic Constitution on the Church)*. Vatican City: Libreria Editrice Vaticana, 1964.

**Classical and Spiritual Writers**
Francis de Sales. *Treatise on the Love of God*. Rockford, IL: TAN Books, 1997.

**Liturgical and Pastoral Sources**
Congregation for Divine Worship. *Directory on Popular Piety and the Liturgy*. Vatican City: Congregation for Divine Worship, 2002.
*Manual of Indulgences*. Washington, DC: USCCB Publishing, 2017.
*The Roman Missal*. Washington, DC: USCCB Publishing, 2011.

# Addenda I & II

**Addendum I: Major Churches and Shrines of the Holy Family**
Archcathedral Basilica of the Holy Family, Częstochowa, Poland. Diocese of Częstochowa archives.
Basilica of the Annunciation, Nazareth, Israel. Custodia Terrae Sanctae archives.
Basilica of the Sagrada Família, Barcelona, Spain. UNESCO World Heritage Centre records.

Cathedral Basilica of the Holy Family, Nairobi, Kenya. Archdiocese of Nairobi archives.

Ukrainian Catholic National Shrine of the Holy Family, Washington, DC. Archeparchy of Philadelphia archives.

## Addendum II: Prayers and Devotions to the Holy Family

Benedict XVI. "Homily for the Feast of the Holy Family." December 30, 2011. Vatican.va.

Carmelite Order. *Manual of Prayer and the Roman Breviary*. Vatican City: Libreria Editrice Vaticana, 1930.

Catechism of the Catholic Church, §2685 (on Family Prayer).

Francis. *Amoris Laetitia*, §318 (Prayer to the Holy Family).

John Paul II. "Prayer for Families." World Meeting of Families, 1994.

*Litany of the Holy Family*. Approved by Pope Leo XIII (1895); indulgence extended by Pope Benedict XV (1921).

*Manual of Indulgences*. Washington, DC: USCCB Publishing, 2017.

*The Roman Missal*. Washington, DC: USCCB Publishing, 2011.

# About the Author

Charlotte Foudy is a Catholic wife, mother, and author whose writing flows from a deep love for Jesus, Mary, and Joseph. She is the founder of Sanctorum Press, where she is dedicated to creating books that renew family life, deepen devotion, and draw readers closer to the heart of Christ.

Charlotte is passionate about helping families rediscover the beauty of the domestic church and the quiet strength found in the hidden life of Nazareth. Her work blends Scripture, tradition, and the lived experience of motherhood, offering readers a gentle and faithful guide to holiness in everyday life.

She lives on the South Shore of Massachusetts with her husband and their children, where she spends her days homeschooling, writing, praying, and striving (imperfectly but joyfully) to make her home a little Nazareth. Much of her writing has been accompanied by quiet cups of green tea and the comforting presence of her beloved cats. She also enjoys spending time outdoors, where the wonders and beauty of nature continually draw her heart back to the Maker of all creation.

# Acknowledgments

With heartfelt gratitude to all who supported this work.
To my husband, Mark, whose steadfast love
and faith have been my strength;
To our children, Michael, Therese, and
Gianna, who daily remind me
of the beauty of family life in Nazareth;
to my many friends, editors, book interior designer,
and readers for their insight and support;
and to the priests and religious who encouraged me to write
and who prayed for this project from its earliest days.
And to the Blessed Virgin Mary and St. Joseph, whose
example shaped every page of this book and whose
prayers sustained me throughout this work.
Above all, I thank you, Jesus, from
whom every good gift comes,
for the grace to complete this work in
His time and for His glory.

*Ad Majorem Dei Gloriam*

# About Sanctorum Press

---

Sanctorum Press is a Catholic publishing apostolate dedicated to supporting prayer, spiritual formation, and a deeper love for Jesus Christ and His Church. We are committed to fostering devotion to the saints, strengthening Catholic identity, and providing faithful resources for families and individuals seeking holiness. Our mission is simple: to produce beautiful, faithful, and spiritually enriching works rooted in Scripture, tradition, and the teachings of the Church. Each book is created with prayer, care, and a desire to encourage holiness in the ordinary ways of daily life.

For updates on future titles, visit:
www.sanctorumpress.com

This book was typeset in EB Garamond and Scotch Modern using Adobe InDesign by the book people at Imprint Media Lab. Published by Sanctorum Press, in a spirit of prayer and devotion to the Holy Family.

www.ingramcontent.com/pod-product-compliance
Lightning Source LLC
Chambersburg PA
CBHW022058120526
44580CB00017B/122/J